# Reconceptualizing Disability in Education

# CRITICAL ISSUES IN DISABILITIES AND EDUCATION

**Series Editor:** Eric Shyman, St. Joseph's College, New York

The social, legal, and political history of persons with disabilities in the United States and internationally has been significant, especially in the areas of social justice, civil rights, and cultural inclusion. This series will focus on various perspectives on issues involving the social, political, and cultural experiences of people with disabilities. Manuscripts in this series will address topics such as: (1) legal developments at both the national and international level; (2) social and cultural models of disability and its outcome on the inclusion and/or exclusion of individuals with disabilities; (3) the benefits and challenges of the current educational system for children and adolescents with disabilities, including specific methodologies and categories of students (e.g., educational approaches for students with Autism Spectrum Disorder, inclusive education for students with disabilities, etc.); (4) philosophical perspectives of special education/education for students with disabilities; and (5) issues regarding transitional support services and approaches to community support for adults with disabilities.

**Titles in Series**

*The Accidental Educator: A Life Contemplating Dis/Ability in Schools and Society* by David J. Connor

*Reconceptualizing Disability in Education* by Luigi Iannacci

# Reconceptualizing Disability in Education

Luigi Iannacci

LEXINGTON BOOKS
*Lanham • Boulder • New York • London*

Published by Lexington Books
An imprint of The Rowman & Littlefield Publishing Group, Inc.
4501 Forbes Boulevard, Suite 200, Lanham, Maryland 20706
www.rowman.com

Unit A, Whitacre Mews, 26-34 Stannary Street, London SE11 4AB

*The Chrysalids*, John Wyndham (1955) is reproduced in chapters 2 and 6 by permission of Paper Lion Ltd. and The John Wyndham US Estate.

Chapter 4 includes excerpts from *The Memory Keeper's Daughter* by Kim Edwards © 2005 by Kim Edwards, used by permission of Viking Books, an imprint of Penguin Publishing Group, a division of Penguin Random House LLC. All rights reserved.

British Library Cataloguing in Publication Information Available

**Library of Congress Cataloging-in-Publication Data**
ISBN 978-1-4985-4275-3 (cloth : alk. paper)
ISBN 978-1-4985-4276-0 (electronic)

♾™ The paper used in this publication meets the minimum requirements of American National Standard for Information Sciences—Permanence of Paper for Printed Library Materials, ANSI/NISO Z39.48-1992.

Printed in the United States of America

# Contents

# A Note from the Series Editor

The *Critical Issues in Disabilities and Education* series seeks to expand the professional discourse regarding the interaction between disability and education in a critical context. This series is deliberately far-reaching and broad so as to allow the most inclusive level of perspectives on the topic as possible. In this work, Luigi Iannacci of Trent University presents a deeply critical analysis of the medical and essentialist models that are dominant in the principles and practices of educating individuals with disabilities. Bringing the overarching ableist perspectives so present in the field into clear focus, Dr. Iannacci elucidates how such practices work to relegate students with disabilities into a marginalized position, acceptable only when they have become rehabilitated to a socially and academically acceptable degree.

To the contrary, Dr. Iannacci puts forth an argument that disability can and should be regarded as an epistemology, identity, and essential factor of diversity upon which a truly enlightened culture thrives. Contextualizing these ideas in a discourse of social justice and human rights, Dr. Iannacci challenges stakeholders in the field to reconsider and replace the medical and essentialist model of disability and inclusion in favor of one that operates out of a set of informed beliefs and practices that focuses on personhood and value of people as they are.

Iannacci uses the concept of literacy or, more precisely, "multiliteracies" as a frame for his argument, thus extending the utility of this perspective for use in the area of educating individuals with disabilities in an inclusive setting. This perspective is particularly forward thinking as the approach toward literacy for individuals is typically characterized by sequenced, mastery-based approaches functioning out of a "deficiency" standpoint. As a result, Dr. Iannacci challenges the reader not to view one's disability as a fixed entity in need of rehabilitation, but rather as an element, or even centrality, of identity which is essential and positively contributive to his or her social functioning. This point is deftly made by employing multiple scholastic and philosophical modalities including critical pedagogy, critical disability theory, post-modernism, and social constructivism. The result is a highly comprehensive and well-structured piece of critical literature.

Essentially, no reader can digest this work without feeling that their preconceptions and beliefs about disability, education, inclusion, and identity has been deeply and foundationally challenged, and will be left even more developed because of it. Even those whose frame of reference is analogous to Dr. Iannacci's will be forced to contend with their deep-seated essentialist leanings, however deep or dormant, and will find themselves restructuring their own thoughts more toward a human rights orientation of inclusive education for individuals with disabilities.

It is my sincere hope that stakeholders of all kinds in the field of disabilities and education avail themselves of this work, including teachers, parents, people with disabilities themselves, educational administrators at all levels, professors, educational researchers, and students. This work would also be particularly appealing to social and cultural theorists across a variety of fields. As the field of Disability Studies in Education (DSE) continues to develop, this work will most certainly become one of its most important contributions.

Eric Shyman, Ed.D.
Editor, Critical Issues in Disabilities and Education

# Foreword

This book provides a critical exploration of problematic discourses, practices and pedagogies that inform how disability is presently understood and responded to within the field of education. One of the central themes the book examines is how the dominant medical/essentialist model of disability (Hosking, 2008) through language, processes, and "interventions" presumed to name and address deficits continues to position disability/people who have a disability as inherently flawed, broken, deficient, and in need of "fixing." In order to forward a social model of disability (Hosking, 2008) and reveal how disability has been problematically constructed and further, offer a much needed reconceptualization that recognizes disability as epistemology, identity, and diversity, the book interrogates and destabilizes ablest grand narratives that dominate every aspect of how disability is linguistically, bureaucratically, procedurally, and pedagogically configured within education. Since the book seeks to explore disability as a way of knowing and to elucidate how people with disabilities can demonstrate these ways of knowing within inclusive education, it is of interest and use to educators teaching at the elementary, secondary, and in-service level as well as graduate students and scholars working in the areas of inclusion, special education, and literacy. The book will also be of interest to parents of children who have a disability. Its perspectives are international and speak to universal issues organizing disability within global educational contexts such as Canada, England, the United States, etc. Ultimately it forwards global human rights for people with disabilities in educational contexts by clarifying and enacting inclusion so that it is not just a model necessitated by legal hierarchy, but rather a set of beliefs and practices based on critical analyses and a reconceptualization of current understandings and responses to disability that prevent inclusion and human rights from being realized.

In order to forward this social justice–focused approach to disability, notions of and intersections between literacy and personhood (as they presently discursively exist) are critically challenged in order to interrogate how print and verbo-centric ideas determine who is allowed to be/considered to be literate and therefore a "thinking" person (Kliewer, 2006). These deeply flawed ideas fail to respond to and provide people with disabilities communication opportunities that allow them to perform their literacies and identities, and as such impede their human rights. A dynamic definition of literacy indicative of multimodal understandings, demonstrations, and engagements with a variety of texts is therefore applied to disability in order to reconceptualize links between literacy and disability and how education can respond to these links in ways that are respectful of diverse communication. The book therefore highlights how literacy can no longer be thought of as singular and informed by the tyranny of the norm, but rather illustrative of what has been termed "multiliteracies" (New London Group, 1996). This is an important application of the multiliteracies literature as these perspectives have been explored in current literacy education research and are at the neophyte stages of reconfiguring mainstream classroom pedagogy, but have not yet informed understandings of or instructional responses to disability. The "special education" field with its long-held beliefs that literacy instruction for those deemed disabled requires a scope and sequenced, fragmented, mastery learning approach continues to utilize impoverished pedagogies (Iannacci, 2018) that deem the disabled unable to participate fully in literacy engagement. The book ultimately challenges these assumptions and many of the discourses that undergird and forward beliefs, practices, pedagogies, policies and processes that devalue and detrimentally respond to disability. This critical examination serves as the impetus for offering reconceptualized perspectives and as such, offers readers both problematics and possibilities.

# Acknowledgments

Thank you to Holly Buchanan and Nicolette Amstutz at Lexington Press for your guidance and support. A great deal of gratitude to Eric Shyman for his initial invitation to write the book and his work as editor. I would like to acknowledge Penny Suhr for her assistance, feedback, and careful editing.

A big thank you to the Malton/Ascension crew and honorary crew members (you know who you are) for years of great friendship. I especially want to thank Lisa Reda for all her support throughout the years.

I want to acknowledge Dr. Rachel Heydon and initial work we did with respect to asset-oriented practices. Thank you for your collegiality and friendship. I also would like to thank Dr. Kathy Hibbert for her ongoing friendship, encouragement, and our vital critical conversations that continue to feed my mind and work. A big thank you to Bente Graham for years of great partnership, friendship, and dedication to teacher education and learners with special needs.

I am indebted to colleagues/friends who provided me with vital feedback. A big thank you to Dr. Rosamund Stooke and Frank Muia for your valuable comments and suggestions as well as Lore, Nicholas, and Marco Muia for your ongoing support.

Thank you to Dr. Sharon Rich for also carefully reading drafts of the book and offering insights and revisions. Your continued mentorship and friendship are extremely important to me. Thank you for years of generosity and consistently believing in me.

Thank you to my parents Aldo and Maria Iannacci and brother Elio Iannacci for all your love.

Finally I want to acknowledge all of the students, teachers, and parents I have worked and learned with and from. This book is because of and dedicated to you. Thank you.

## Chapter One

# Personal, Professional, Theoretical, and Methodological Perspectives

As a twenty-five-year veteran educator who has taught general and special education and currently teaches at the post-secondary level, I have a personal and professional interest in disability, diversity, and education. I currently teach and coordinate courses that focus on language and literacy, cultural, and linguistic diversity and learners with special needs at the pre-service level at Trent University in Peterborough, Ontario, Canada. I have also taught graduate courses at Trent and for other universities across Canada on inclusion and literacy (as it relates to students with disabilities), critical narrative research, curriculum evaluation, multiliteracies and identities and reconceptualist approaches to early childhood education. My book publications have focused on disability/diversity (Heydon & Iannacci, 2008) and reconceptualizing early childhood education (Iannacci & Whitty, 2009). Other research I have published has focused on first and second language and literacy learning, critical multiculturalism, critical dis/ability studies, early childhood education, critical narrative research, and ethics. I mention all of this because my entire career has in many ways been informed by my past and this book is written as a result of significant experiences I have had. As a child I was placed in a special education classroom and have firsthand knowledge of what it means to be assigned pedagogy and an identity based on ascribed deficiencies. All of this personal, professional, research, and teaching experience drives me to author this book.

I share my story to firmly establish my presence from the onset. In doing so, I further the notion that "objective" research that pretends to ignore the subjective is neither possible nor productive. Like Diane Reay (1998), I believe that "all research is in one way or another autobiographical or else the avoidance of autobiography" (p. 2). This notion has resonated with me throughout the sometimes painful process of confronting and reflecting on my autobiography while developing research. As these experiences have fostered critical questions that shape this book, it is necessary to share some of them in order to provide a background and context and make explicit how the personal becomes manifest in knowledge formation. Revealing the strong links between who I am, what I've lived and how this influences my work, highlights the importance of researcher self-disclosure and reflexivity, which is integral to developing validity and an ethical stance.

Ethics is a central concern throughout this book and therefore essential to foster. This is especially important given the book's focus and the fact that the ways in which disability has been taken up in education has been dominated by policies, practices, and research that have been detrimental to students and fueled by unquestioned beliefs that have served to forward deficit thinking and pathologizing. This book intends to destabilize these taken-for-granted and unquestioned dominant narratives about disability as they have manifested in education and provide critical conversation about how students with disabilities are understood and provided for in educational contexts. The conversation serves as the impetus for a much needed transformation of education provided to students with disabilities. I begin by exploring the events that have led to my need to further this critical conversation and offer alternatives.

## POSITIONING: PERSONAL AND PROFESSIONAL PERSPECTIVES

Part of the postwar wave of immigrants from Italy, my parents immigrated to Canada as young adults. They married and settled in Toronto. I was born in 1970. From a very early age I knew that they valued education and lamented the fact that they were never given the opportunity to pursue theirs. Therefore, my success within school was extremely important to them.

Most of my formative years were spent at home with my mom, singing Italian songs, dancing to Italian music, eating Italian food, and speaking Italian. When my dad came home, the three of us filled the house with conversation and stories. This was the life, language, and culture they gave me.

The memories that vividly come back to me as I started my grade one year begin with the smell of the classroom. As I walked in, the scent of books permeated the room. The first-born child of Italian immigrant parents, I was beginning grade one. I was a reason for sacrifice. Although I couldn't articulate it, I could feel that I had to learn how to read those books and achieve. I had to love school, because I loved my parents. It was imperative that I not disappoint them, and yet this is what I felt I did very quickly.

Almost immediately after the start of that year, my first language became problematic for the school. My English was not nearly as well developed as that of other students my age. I was not concerned at first since I was too busy pursuing activities that interested me such as repeatedly listening to *Peter Pan* on audio tape at the listening center. Over time it became ever more apparent to the teacher that my English was preventing me from fully understanding what was occurring in the classroom. In contrast to my behavior at home, I was extremely quiet and never wanted to be singled out. When I was asked questions, I felt a surge of anxiety run through my body since I knew I couldn't possibly have the right answer. There was much that that I wanted to say, but could not in English. When spoken to directly by the teacher, I would sit stoically as my face turned red and melted in the heat of my confusion and embarrassment.

The school's immediate response to my difficulties was to place me in a special education class where I was subjected to intense doses of fragmented English language learning. The dissemination of vast numbers of phonics sheets was standard practice. Like compliant circus elephants, my classmates and I were given unshelled peanuts every time we completed a worksheet correctly or gave a correct response in English. I distinctly remember one of my classmates becoming so frustrated with these deadening sessions that he violently spat on the floor. The teacher gave him a lecture about how "we" do not spit on the floor in classrooms in Canada. Spitting was strictly an outdoor activity and even then was disgusting. He was sent to find the janitor so he could borrow his mop and clean up his protest. I sat there in silence, feeling guilty about how much I appreciated his act and envied his momentary escape.

My parents were called to the school and told to begin speaking to me in English at home. Having been made aware of my problems, they became alarmed and concerned. Since they wanted their son to succeed and be granted opportunities they never had, they were willing to follow the school's request. At home we began to speak English more frequently. There were fewer Italian songs and conversation became strained as phonics workbooks infiltrated my home life.

Throughout this, I felt an overwhelming sense of guilt. My problems at school were because of my failures. I failed to live up to my parents' and teachers' expectations. I failed to acquire English and that meant having to go to a "special" class instead. My failure also meant that we could not speak Italian at home as we used to, and that I was stupid. I spent the next two years eating peanuts, attempting to finish one phonics workbook after another, having difficulties learning English and feeling stupid.

During this time, and in spite of my own experiences in special education, an incident occurred that had a profound effect on me in terms of thinking about people who have disabilities. I was in the car with my dad and saw a man in a wheelchair being pushed by another man. It was clear that the man had severe physical disabilities as his limbs were contorted and spastic. I watched him closely at the stop light as he and his caregiver crossed the street. As we drove I asked my dad, "How does he work?"

My dad looked at me with slight annoyance and said, "What you mean?"

I added, "He can't work so what does he do?"

My dad sharply responded, "He live."

I pressed on. "But how does he live if he doesn't have a job?"

With his voice raised he very quickly spat out, "You live. You don't work. We take care of you. He live and we take care of him. We pay tax and some goes to people who can't work."

I interjected, "*We* pay?!"

At this point he lost all patience, pulled the car over to the side of the road, and put it in park. He shifted his body so that he was directly facing me and making eye contact. He then yelled, "It's your business he can't work? Why you care when you don't work? Mine your business." He then sighed exasperatedly, turned to face the steering wheel, put the car in drive, and speedily drove us home. We sat in silence and never talked about the incident or the man in the wheelchair again.

When I was ten, my family went to Italy. We went to my father's home where I was going to meet my Nonno and Nonna for the first time. I entered the house and was greeted with a big tight hug from my Nonna. I felt the tight grip of one of her arms and noticed the other was limp. She began speaking to me excitedly but I couldn't make out what she was saying. My dad stepped in and translated. It wasn't because she was speaking Italian; I could still understand Italian completely. It was her speech. She mumbled loudly and expressively but one side of her face did not move. No one had told me she had a stroke years prior that left her without the use of one side of her body. When she walked she dragged her leg and propelled herself with the other. My father and grandfather could make out what she was saying as they had experience doing so. I was amazed at how they could understand her so easily when I couldn't make out a word.

As time went by it became clearer to me that my dad's anger and irritation in the car was very personal and that I had offended him given his own experiences with his mother. How could he not be upset at his son who reduced the value of people with disabilities down to whether they worked for money?

It was not until grade six that I began to make gains at school. I associated these gains and the fact that I was no longer in special education with my expanding English language skills and the rejection of my Italian language and culture. I began to feel that the more "English" I made myself become, the better I did at school.

High school in contrast became a time of emerging pride in my cultural and linguistic background and undoing some of the assimilation I had previously experienced. Although this was an empowering time, feelings of intellectual inadequacy and deficiency remained.

All of these experiences shaped my decision to become a teaching assistant, a teacher, and eventually a special education teacher. I wanted to use my experiences to ensure that students would not have to undergo what I did. Unfortunately, I noticed very quickly that specialized support (whether it be ESL or special education) was inadequate and what was offered presented language in isolated and fragmented ways, which I knew to be problematic and ineffective through personal experience and later, my teaching degree.

The conservative government elected the year after I started teaching had caused a great deal of upheaval in the school system in the years leading up to my decision to pursue graduate school. I witnessed further deterioration of services and support provided to struggling students and grew increasingly concerned about decisions being made related to this lack of support.

In my last year of teaching before taking a leave of absence to do a Master of Education degree, I was invited to a district meeting to examine and discuss several literacy programs and select one for possible use in our school district. One of the products, *Open Court*, was phonics intensive, heavily scripted and artificially sequenced. It reminded me of the endless workbooks I had to complete as a special education student and completely opposed what I had learned about effective literacy instruction. The publishers declared that the program was hugely successful and widely used in the United States.

As we discussed which program should be considered for the district, I became progressively more frustrated. I knew and had worked with many of the teachers involved in this decision making process. None of them lived in the area and commuted from middle and upper middle-class neighborhoods. Although well intentioned, they firmly believed that *Open Court* should be purchased on the premise that "*these* kids needed" prescriptive, decoding-focused direct instruction given area test results. When I had an opportunity to talk, I asked committee members whether they would want their own children to use these materials in the schools they attended. A few of them answered "no" while others remained silent. They added that their children didn't need such a program because they did not have the same problems students in the area where we taught were having with literacy. The implications of their assumptions and the pedagogical quality of the materials were never questioned. Although I fought to change minds, most of the committee members who represented different schools decided to purchase *Open Court*.

Throughout this time I began to wonder how my story could be used to combat school decisions and ministry mandates that I believed to be harmful to students. I wondered how I could use what I knew about how detrimental these practices were and felt that my underdeveloped voice remained mostly unheard and of little consequence. Graduate school would change all of this.

When I began my Master of Education degree in 1997, I took courses that I believed would help me gain an understanding of how my story could be used to transform what I had personally and professionally experienced. The courses I took gave me the language and specific knowledge that would allow me to discuss my story with an informed, clear and developed voice. I left graduate school with a better understanding of myself and how to provide and advocate for students. Although I realized that my initial goal of being able to use my story to facilitate change would take time, the experience had developed my voice in ways that I could not have as an elementary school student or teacher.

Following graduate school I became a special education resource classroom teacher, which meant teaching and running a Junior/Intermediate (grades five through eight) comprehensive class. The self-contained class housed students who had been formally identified as having an exceptionality through the Identification and Placement Review Committee (IPRC) process. Students spent 50 percent of their day in the class for literacy, numeracy, and social skills instruction and the remainder of the day in their regular grade classroom for all other areas of the curriculum. The class was both challenging and rewarding. There were, however, a number of students learning English as a second language (ESL) who had been identified as learning disabled and placed within the class. While reviewing Ontario Student Records (OSRs), I discovered that none of the ESL students in my class had ever received ESL support. They were placed in special education classes or provided with special education support shortly after immigration to Canada and subsequently formally identified as having a disability. Considering my personal experiences, the work I had just done during my Master's degree, and the questions I was left with, I found the situation ironic and disturbing. I also realized, however, that because of my personal and professional background, these students would receive instruction that did not resemble dominant special education "interventions" that were both fragmented and based on perceived deficiencies. Although far from ideal or appropriate, my students' identification and placement protected them from receiving no support whatsoever and this was vital given the educational context they were immersed in that privileged and focused on standardized curriculum and testing.

This protection was especially evident when I was told that despite their formal identification, all of the grade six students in my special education class would have to write the Education Quality and Accountability Office

(EQAO) provincial standardized test. Although grade six EQAO testing had been in place for approximately 3–4 years, exemptions were unclear, and further, a system-wide belief that all students would have to write the test was dominant. Therefore, a few months before the test was to take place, I arranged a meeting with the principal to explain why all of the grade six students in my class needed to be exempt from taking the test, and outlined alternative programming for them. We reviewed each of the students on a case-by-case basis and once I provided a rationale and reviewed their documentation, he agreed to exempt the students from participating. Being informed and understanding how to navigate through these situations was something I felt my graduate degree prepared me for. I was no longer silent, nor could I be silenced.

Incidents such as these throughout the years I taught the special education class validated my choices and healed some of my past scars. As personally and professionally satiating as teaching the class was, eventually I knew it was time to formally explore questions cultivated as a result of my personal, professional and academic experiences. With this in mind, I decided to pursue a PhD in education.

The PhD continued to shape and forward my thinking. I was fortunate to work with a gifted supervisor and many incredible fellow students/colleagues that influenced and further developed my voice/work. Events and incidents that demonstrate their collegiality and impact are too numerous to recount. What is necessary to share is a vital moment where my thinking about disability and people with disabilities shifted in necessary and profound ways. As I wrote my dissertation, I struggled with feelings of inadequacy. My institutional identity as a "special education kid" haunted me. Internalized links between disability and deficiency went largely unquestioned until I encountered this quote from Bernadette Baker that made me realize that my unresolved issues with respect to being a special education student had prevented me from critically understanding the problematic ways disability has been constructed and responded to in education.

> . . . critiques of cultural bias in special education can inadvertently recirculate the forbidden relationship between disability and desire, that is, how disability, whether it is analyzed as "biomedical" or "socially constituted through relationships," *must not be desired*, how it is used as nomenclature for a negative ontology and posed as a way of being that at all cost ought to be avoided. Where a critique of labeling or overrepresentation turns on the view that "normal" students are really being mislabeled and made closer on a scale to "genuinely" "disabled" students, then it does not undermine the presumptions that "it's better to be dead than disabled." If, as Campbell (2000, p. 307) has argued, the construction/governing of disability and all the compulsion toward

an ableist normativity are in fact achieved by the continual reiteration of technologies as "salvific signifiers" holding out the promise of "able-bodiedness"
then both the hunt to identify disability, and some versions of its critique, leave
unproblematized this promise. (Baker, 2002, p. 685)

Baker's words and the work of many others shifted my thinking in profound ways and made me question my discourse and the nature of my work.
It became apparent that my opposition to students being misidentified as
disabled was not solely about the problematic ways culturally and linguistically diverse students were positioned in educational contexts such as schools,
but also about an ablest internalized aversion to disability that began in my
childhood and remained largely unquestioned. These shifts in my thinking
changed my work and changed me. As these perspectives influence the
contents of this book, they must be explored and made explicit since they
inform what is offered throughout subsequent chapters.

## BACKGROUND AND THEORETICAL PERSPECTIVES

In this book I draw on a variety of personal, professional experiences as
well as research data to critically address questions regarding philosophical,
epistemological, pedagogical, organizational, economic and leadership issues related to disability in education. I ground the book in reconceptualist
theorizing and therefore use a pastiche of perspectives (Iannacci & Whitty,
2009) including critical disability theory, post-modernism, critical theory,
critical pedagogy, social constructivism and multiliteracies theory to explore
what is currently taken for granted about disability and those ascribed disabled identities within education. Reconceptualist approaches stress the
importance of deconstructing the ways in which dominant discourses shape
interactions and practices in order to prevent the reinscription and furthering
of inequitable and coercive relations of power (Cummins, 2001). This is a
critical project that "invokes a tradition of curricular theorizing that sees as its
goal the social transformation and reconstruction of educational institutions"
(Iannacci & Whitty, 2009, p. 22). The book therefore draws on and is
indebted to the reconceptualist movement in curriculum studies founded by
people such as Bill Pinar and Madeleine Grumet among others.

Reconceptualizing disability is especially necessary at this point in time
as the "hunt for disability" (Baker, 2002) and the fallout from this hunt have
led to the "proliferation of categories of educational disability" (p. 676)
and a subsequent significant increase in the number of students assigned a
"disability label at an earlier age than in the past" (p. 678). The "swarming
effect"—the name that Baker (2002) gave "the hunt for and diagnosis

of disability as a negative ontology that schools actively seek to name" (p. 679)—necessitates that attention be paid to how disability is conceptualized, provided for, and understood as curriculum, relationships, and pedagogy have been primary factors in framing the ways that students have been constructed and positioned within education (Triplett, 2007). As Heydon & Iannacci (2008) have pointed out, questions of disability are prerequisites for all educational conversations as what to teach or how to teach can never be adequately addressed without an understanding of who students are.

Reconceptualizing disability at this time is also imperative as few inroads have been made within the field of curriculum studies insofar as examining constructions of disability and children deemed disabled (Heydon & Iannacci, 2008). A content analysis of ten years of issues of four prominent, peer-reviewed, international curriculum studies' journals found that the journals included only between one and five articles that directly and/or peripherally referred to issues of disability or to curriculum for disabled students (Heydon & Iannacci, 2008). This minimal attention or exclusion "has meant that there are limited spaces in education that trouble what it means to be able or disabled or that question the curricula of disabled students" (p. 48). The field therefore has continued to support the special education–regular education binary that has led to unchallenged special education models and pedagogy.

A large-scale analysis of four major electronic databases searched using the term "reading disabilities" revealed similar gaps and absences and a view of learning disabilities as psychometric and biomedical in nature (Moffatt, 2006). Of the 760 abstracts published between January 2000 and mid-October 2005 that were found in the search, 99 percent of them accepted the concept of "reading disability" and did not challenge it from a critical perspective or consider "reading disability" as a social construct. Instead, 92 percent of the abstracts conceptualized intelligence/learning as things that can be easily assessed through standardized assessment tools. The data set also demonstrated how 40 percent of the abstracts conceptualized reading disabilities as connected to phonological awareness. The idea that reading dis/abilities are the result of bio-medical deficits/gifts was present in 25 percent of the data thus reinforcing the idea of dis/ability as something within a child's body. Finally, 25 percent of the articles located difficulties/success with literacy learning in students' family histories, nutrition, motivations for reading, orthographic awareness, physical health, school attendance, socio-economic class, and available learning materials (Moffatt, 2006).

Research I conducted with my colleague Bente Graham (2010) critically analyzed discourses present in surveys completed by teacher candidates before they began their initial teacher education program as well as a survey and focus groups conducted after they finished it. Throughout their Bachelor of Education, participating teacher candidates were exposed to curriculum that critically explored notions of literacy and disability. Data demonstrated multi-faceted and contradictory perspectives. Although teacher candidates' views of literacy had expanded and were indicative of multiliteracies perspectives that see literacy as a social practice, their specific understandings about disability continued to be informed by a medical, deficit model as they described disability in relation to norms identified in government texts and school board mandated evaluations. Disabilities therefore were understood as an impairment, a deficit, and/or a disorder. All of the above findings demonstrate that the "symbolic complex," a constellation of terms, concepts, practices (Danforth, 2009) and "cultural analysis" (McDermott & Varenne, 1995) required to fully consider disability within education, has yet to be realized. A reconceptualist approach utilizes a theoretical pastiche to destabilize dominant discourses and provides a way to address this necessary complexity. Critical disability theory, one of the perspectives drawn on throughout this book, is necessary to facilitate destabilization.

## CRITICAL DISABILITY THEORY

At its core, critical disability theory views disability "as a cultural fabrication" (McDermott & Varenne, 1995, p. 323) and therefore a social construct rather than an inherent flaw. Research from critical disability studies has specifically been concerned with interrogating the language used in relation to those identified as disabled and in the context of disability. This interrogation examines the impact of normative discourses (e.g., able/disabled binaries) and the ways in which these binaries reproduce/evoke/draw on other discourses (Pothier & Devlin, 2006). As such, disabilities are conceptualized as something created from what we as a society do and what we consider worthy of doing. Thomas (2004) further explains, "Disability is a form of social oppression involving the social imposition of restrictions of activity on people with impairments and the socially engendered undermining of their psycho-emotional well-being" (p. 580). In short, "disabilities are less the property of persons than they are moments in a cultural focus" (McDermott & Varenne, 1995, p. 323).

In terms of educational contexts, it stands to reason that "no student can have LD [learning disabilities] on his or her own. It takes a complex system of interactions performed in just the right way, at the right time, on the stage we call school" (Dudley-Marling, 2004, p. 489). Padden & Humphries (1988) similarly argue that "being able or unable . . . does not emerge as significant in itself; instead it takes on significance in the context of other sets of meaning to which the child has been exposed" (in McDermott & Varenne, 1995, p. 325). Titchkosky (2007) further explains:

"Disability" . . . is a process of meaning-making that takes place somewhere and is done by somebody. Whenever disability is perceived, spoken, or even thought about, people mean it in some way. The ways that disability comes to have meaning have something to teach us about our life-worlds. Understanding disability as a site where meaning is enacted not only requires conceptualizing disability as a social accomplishment, it also means developing an animated sense of that which enacts these meanings. (p.12)

As disability is "made by culture," it must also be understood as a text that can be read and written about and a "prime space to reread and rewrite a culture's makings" (Titchkosky, 2007, p. 6). The language assigned to people identified as disabled and the ways in which this language compromises their personhood and reifies and centers their identities in relation to their defined and measured deficiencies is therefore a central concern and an important focus of this book as so much of the "disability discourse serves something other than the interests of disabled people . . . [as it] is made viable as a metaphor to express only that which is unwanted and that which is devastatingly inept" (Titchkosky, 2007, p. 5). Deconstructing and destabilizing this dominant discourse is a necessary political act that researchers and activists working with/in critical disability studies have taken on.

Disability is politicized. While individual, medical, and deficit models continue to dominate thinking *about* disabled people, critical disability studies calls for counter-hegemony *with* disabled people. Alternative discourses. A reassessment of the dialectical split of (impaired) body/mind in society. . . . Clearly, then, an engagement with pedagogy involves a deconstruction of disabling pedagogies or pedagogies of exclusion. (Goodley, 2007, p. 319)

Although these goals, aims, and foci have been neglected within educational research and practice and absent from the "discourses of critical pedagogy" (Gabel, 2002, as cited in Goodley, 2007, p. 318), new approaches and perspectives are at the neophyte stages of acceptance and application.

## AN ASSET-ORIENTED APPROACH TO DISABILITY

In response to this troubling positioning of disability, new approaches have begun to develop. Rejecting the deficit model that has remained dominant within education in relation to disability, Heydon & Iannacci (2008) explored asset-oriented ways of seeing and responding to disability and diversity. An asset-oriented approach vehemently rejects "at-risk" discourses while positioning students as "at-promise" (Swadener & Lubeck, 1995). This approach recognizes and builds on students' "funds of knowledge (FoK)" (Moll,

1992) and therefore views learners as able, and in possession of literacies and social, cognitive, artistic, emotional, cultural, linguistic, affective, epistemological, etc., resources rather than lacking literacy, deficient, or disordered. In this way, Heydon & Iannacci (2008) apply and extend the original intent and definition of FoK to disability/people with disabilities in order to facilitate an asset-oriented repositioning of disability that highlights its present discursive configuration as a consequence of social/institutional rather than individual deficits. This application of FoK to disability is just beginning to emerge (Kim & Aquino, 2017). As such, an asset-oriented approach that draws on and applies the FoK concept furthers this necessary application.

Although reconceptualizing disability in ways that are asset-oriented is essential, the approach also understands that "how students are discursively constructed has material effects" (Paugh & Dudley-Marling, 2011, p. 7). As such, language assigned to students deemed disabled and the ways in which this language compromises their personhood and reifies their identities in relation to their defined and measured deficiencies in learning contexts is a central concern of an asset-oriented approach. Asset-oriented perspectives further contribute to the emerging body of literature that is just beginning to work at destabilizing the monolith of disability as it appears in and is significant to education. It is necessary therefore to not only destabilize taken for granted notions of disability within education, but also offer practices and possibilities that operationalize how education can respond to disability in ways that are truly inclusive. This is especially important given the fact that Hehir (2002) has noted that ableism, defined as the "devaluation of disability" (p. 1), has been pervasive in education. This pervasiveness has meant that many educators continue to believe that "it is preferable for disabled students to do things in the same manner of nondisabled kids" (p. 3). These views of course perpetuate the norm/non-norm divide that positions disability as a deficit and something that must be fixed or changed to conform to norms. Hehir (2002) points out that these prevailing prejudices have a negative impact on both the identity and life course options of students with disabilities.

## METHODOLOGICAL PERSPECTIVES

Critical narrative research (CNR) is used to address key questions, concerns, and foci about disability throughout this book. CNR is an emerging genre of inquiry that frequently border crosses a variety of theoretical orientations (e.g., social constructivist, critical, decolonial) and borrows from ethnographic traditions while remaining aware of its colonial underpinnings (Clair, 2003). It also combines a variety of sets of criteria for evaluating its validity (i.e., social constructivist, artistic, and critical change criteria) (Patton, 2002).

Much of the content of a critical narrative inquiry "draws from critical theories, in that they embody a critique of prevailing structures and relationships of power and inequity in a relational context" (p. 21). The "criticalness" of narrative research must be further explained to distinguish the methodology from the mere telling of stories. The term "critical" is used to describe "culture, language, and participation as issues of power in need of critique with the intent of emendation or alteration in the direction of social justice and participatory democracy" (Moss, 2004, p. 363) and as such has been added to narrative research in order "to signify this explicitly political project" (Burdell & Swadener, 1999, p. 21). CNR is therefore concerned with culture, language, and participation as issues of power in need of critique with the intent of change in the direction of social justice (Moss, 2004). Taken for granted relations of power experienced by those constructed as the Other are interrogated through an analysis of observed phenomenon (Iannacci, 2007).

The style of engagement CNR develops is also contingent on the production of a variety of text forms that include but are not restricted to poetry, prose, as well as traditional field and research notes. The texts that are developed and offered throughout a critical narrative borrow from ethnography and literature. Aesthetic representation is one of the ways the postcolonial turn in research has addressed the limits of ethnography (Clair, 2003). As such, cultural practices expressed within CNR assume a variety of aesthetic forms influenced by and commensurate with critical and postcolonial theoretical dispositions seeking to uncover what has been taken for granted or deemed "neutral" while resisting the idea that there is a single "truth," a notion that has been reinforced by and criticized for being present within traditional conceptualizations of ethnography (Clair, 2003). CNR rejects the idea of universal truths and does not profess to make claims in the knowledge it constructs (DeLuca, 2000).

As demonstrated at the beginning of this chapter and the offering of my story, CNR explores connections between the researcher and his/her research and as such, demands that researchers remain "autobiographically conscious" throughout the research process (Viruru & Cannella 2001, p. 168). Critical narrative researchers are therefore deeply interested in exploring the relationship between "their life experience and the theoretical underpinnings of their scholarship" (Grant, 1999, p. 2 in Burdell & Swadener, 1999, p. 24). As critical researchers, they "describe ways in which their life histories, political involvement, moments of insight, and desire to work in alliances for social change made an impact on their research agenda and professional growth" (p. 24). It is therefore essential for CNR researchers to fully implicate themselves within their inquiry and then present and investigate their storied constructions of experience as pluralistic, un-unified, contradictory, problematic and perhaps even incoherent (Miller, 1998). In short, they "conduct research in a way that demystifies the systems of reasoning behind why they do what they do" (Grant, 1999, p. 1). The "resultant knowing that is discovered is multidimensional, partial, and critical" (Moss, 2004, p. 364). These approaches to knowledge formation resist colonial traditions of inquiry that have constructed identities, the Other, and phenomena in general as unified and in contrast, are concerned with uncovering the subtleties, complexities and biases that come with representing culture (Clair, 2003).

My personal and professional experiences corroborate the view that research should be conceptualized to advance this "process of continual self-conscious critique" (Viruru & Cannella, 2001, p. 168). This demands a methodology that resists the pat, the simplistic and the predictive in favor of one that recognizes the complexity and multiplicity of lived experience and the importance of fully disclosing the subjectivity of the research process. In being committed to this critical understanding of narrated experience, research voices that may further call into question links between my personal experiences, biases, and research observations and interpretations are explored and made explicit. As such, multivocality, the questioning of previous assumptions of empirical authority and the interrogation of the construction of subjectivity (Burdell & Swadener, 1999), is extremely salient to CNR. Bakhtin's (1981) notion of "dialogic listening" is helpful in conceptualizing how it may be fostered. Leiblich et al. (1998) identify "three voices" that must all be heard and reconciled in furthering the dialogism Bakhtin describes as imperative to critical narrative research. These voices are that of the narrator, the theoretical framework and the voice that emerges from a "reflexive monitoring of the act of reading and interpretation, that is, self-awareness of the decision process of drawing conclusions" (p.10). This reconciliation does not necessitate cohesiveness or validation of my voice and theoretical proclivities, but rather is intended to foster multiplicity within the narrated accounts I will be providing in order to "splinter the dogmatism of a single tale" (Grumet, 1991, in Miller, 1998, p. 149). These critical perspectives, developed as storied accounts of my personal, professional and researched experiences, are interrogated and challenged. Story, then, will be used as the impetus for reconceptualizing what a society, a profession or a researcher has intentionally or inadvertently communicated as unproblematic, objective or "true." Reconceptualization is realized through a process of construction, deconstruction, and re-construction. This is a "threefold mimesis" that "refers to three domains: a past, a present mediating act, and a future. Ricoeur uses the subscripts 1, 2, 3 to identify the different mimesis (Herda, 1999, p. 76). Mimesis 1 is the world as presented in narrative form (construction). Mimesis 2 occurs through reflection about and distancing from prejudices and pre-understandings (deconstruction). The reflexive monitoring Leiblich et al. (1998) identify is crucial to this stage. Mimesis 3 applies these insights to a refigured future (reconceptualization) in an effort to put forward an "opening up of possible new worlds" (p. 77). In other words, a discussion and critical examination of what is and why it is first occurs, followed by a re-visioning of what can be.

## DATA, ANALYSIS AND QUESTIONS

In developing my arguments, I use ethnographic, case study, and autobiographical data to construct narratives then deconstruct them through critical reflection focused on discourses and power relations that inform what is presently dominant with respect to disability within education. Critical incidents, interviews, documents, artifacts, etc. are drawn together and narratively presented to explore how disability is presently configured in language, identification and placement processes, discourses, pedagogies, and interactions with students deemed disabled as well as their parents. This narrative approach aims to make what is being argued and offered accessible and clear to the reader. Critical narrative research is methodologically the basis for data analysis/presentation and commensurate with the book's aims, goals, and foci as it is situated in the critical paradigm and focused on interrogating culture, language, and power in order to develop social justice based agendas and practices. Again, reconceptualized understandings are developed as a result of a "threefold mimesis" (Ricoeur, 1992). The process involves constructing the world in narrative form, deconstructing what has been narrated, and finally providing reconceptualized insights to refigure a future. Reconceptualization is thus fostered through a process of construction, deconstruction, and re-construction. The ultimate goal of this process is to offer alternative ways of thinking, being, and doing that forward a human rights focused social model of disability that sees as its mandate the amelioration of people with disabilities.

In summary, in the book I address the following questions and concerns:

- What discursive, epistemological, philosophical, pedagogic, leadership shifts are necessary to reconceptualize disability within education?
- What are practices, pedagogies and processes that facilitate this reconceptualization?

These questions informed by an understanding of disability as socially situated and constructed have been recognized as a goal for researchers and activists working within critical disability studies to pursue. Titchkosky (2007) points out:

Critical attention to how disability is and is not read and written today is one way to participate in the disability studies project of destabilization. Such attention can lead us toward reading and writing disability differently, and provide for the possibility of developing new relations to the cultural values that ground the various appearances and disappearances of disability in everyday life. (p. 5)

## ORGANIZATION OF THE BOOK

The remainder of the book is organized in ways that address major areas and issues as they pertain to disability in education in order to foster destabilization. Chapter two therefore explores a reconceptualized understanding of inclusion that interrogates present misunderstandings of the model in terms of the language, processes, and discourses that continue to problematically frame disability in ways that prevent inclusion from being genuinely realized. The chapter presents a reconceptualized view of inclusion based on critical analyses of these processes, discourses, and language.

Chapter three extends this conversation by critically examining disability as philosophy and epistemology and therefore identifies principles and understandings that foster necessary shifts in how disability is spoken of, thought of, and responded to within education. The chapter explores disability as a way of knowing, a resource and an identity in order to demonstrate a marked difference from current discourses that position it as defectiveness.

Chapter four examines intersections between literacy and disability and uses multiliteracies perspectives to reconfigure these intersections within education in ways that are respectful of and responsive to the literacies people with disabilities possess. Pedagogical approaches informed by multiliteracies perspectives are provided as a counter narrative to the limited and limiting understandings of literacy/literacy pedagogy currently assigned to people who have disabilities within education. What follows is a critical examination of economics and ethics as they relate to disability within education as this issue directly affects pedagogy. The chapter therefore ends by critically exploring the current economics of "special education" and how it positions disability. Critical questions regarding identification and placement processes, official documents and their relationship to "spececonomics" and instruction are examined in order to develop ethical praxis.

Chapter five demonstrates the importance of providing educators and community agency workers at all levels opportunities to understand parental perspectives. Power, privilege, pathologizing, and expertism are explored as hindrances that prevent educators, schools, and community agencies from fully developing ethical, respectful, and reciprocal interactions and relationships with parents of students who have disabilities. This critical discussion then provides the background for shifts in perspectives and practices that facilitate a reconceptualization of disability within education as it relates to students and the parents of students with special needs.

The final chapter of the book provides a summary of reconceptualized understandings of and approaches to disability within education. This chapter synthesizes the previous five chapters in order to clearly identify and define reconceptualized approaches to disability within the field of education. Practices, processes, and pedagogies will be brought together to provide the reader with a final overall schema for understanding and responding to disability in ways that facilitate a reconceptualization of current notions and practices within education.

Given the theoretical lenses drawn on and recurring points made throughout the book about the need for context-embedded instruction (Cummins, 2001), the book moves from researcher/writer positioning to theory and methodology which then provides the reader with a context and rationale for the questions being explored. In order for these questions to be addressed, dominant discourses, language, laws, and processes that govern disability and inclusion are first critically interrogated. Narratives and critical analyses of narratives are then offered and interwoven in subsequent chapters in order to illustrate major theoretical, epistemological, and philosophical points. The book unfolds accumulatively as chapters build off of previous content and narratives. A sustained exploration of practices with respect to instruction in chapter four builds upon all of the chapters that come before it. Chapter five similarly is designed and placed where it is in order to coalesce and further illuminate all that comes before it so that the voice of parents of children with disabilities is heard before practices are drawn out of and from their lived experiences. All of this then enables chapter 6 to occur in ways that are now meaningful to the reader. Without reading the chapters in order, the reconceptualization of disability in education offered does not have the same impact and runs the risk of being understood as bullet points or lists of "have tos" or "how tos." This is contradictory to the point of the book and indicative of problematic and dominant approaches in education that rely on and look for quick fixes and laundry lists of things to do to address "problems." In contrast, the book ultimately aims to read and write disability critically and differently (Titchkosky, 2007) within education. This is a necessary reconceptualization of disability as what a disability is and who people with disabilities are requires critical and thoughtful consideration in order to forward social justice and human rights focused educators and educational systems.

# Chapter Two

# Discourses, Language, Laws, and Processes that Govern Disability and Inclusion

The Devil sends Deviations among us to weaken us and tempt us away from Purity. Sometimes he is clever enough to make a nearly perfect imitation, so we have always to be on the look-out for the mistake he has made, however small, and when we see one it must be reported at once. You'll remember that in the future, won't you?

—*The Chrysalids*, John Wyndham, 1955

In order to fully understand present mis/understandings of inclusion and how and why they have been taken up in education, it is first essential to critically explore how disability has been historically and discursively created and organized. Such an unpacking and disrupting of disability is necessary in order for educators to experience and become aware of complex understandings of inclusion that avoid reinscribing notions of disability as monolithic, deviance, or deficit (Fraser & Shields, 2010). As stated in chapter one, Critical Disability Theory (CDT) may help to destabilize dominant notions/discourses of disability and reconfigure the taken for granted about its nature. CDT forwards a social model of disability that views it as a socially mediated, social construct (Hosking, 2008). "Disability" is therefore neither a fossilized, neutral "thing" nor an inherent flaw. This understanding of disability requires an interrogation of the language and notions applied to those identified as disabled in the context of dis/ability and critically questions the impact of normative discourses (e.g., able/disabled binaries) and the ways in which these binaries reproduce/evoke/draw on other discourses (e.g., developmentalism, standardization, neoliberalism, etc.) (Pothier & Devlin, 2006). The language assigned to people with disabilities and the ways in which this language compromises their personhood and reifies their identities in relation to their defined and measured deficiencies is therefore a central concern of CDT since "disability" is ultimately a text that can be read and written about. Critical attention to how disability is read and written is therefore one way to participate in the disability studies project of destabilization. Such attention can lead toward reading and writing disability differently, and "provide for the possibility of developing new relations to the cultural values that ground the various appearances and disappearances of disability in everyday life" (Titchkosky, 2007, p. 5). If educators are to develop these "new relations" as they forward inclusion and inclusive practices they will need to understand and be guided by a social model of disability. Dolmage (2014) states:

> The fact that disability is so naturally and habitually associated with negativity in our society means that we cannot neglect to question these natural habits, and we cannot forget that the pause, reflection, and reconsideration we might engender will themselves be critical and creative opportunities (p. 33).

Therefore, understanding the history of disability, the etymology and creation of "normal" and societal movements informed by this history and construction is vital to undergirding these new relations, criticality and creativity.

"Disability" and societal responses to people with disabilities have had a troubled and troubling past influenced by a myriad of problematic[1] myths (Dolmage, 2014) and replete with human rights abuses. Throughout the sixteenth century, for example, people with disabilities were thought of as demonic and subjected to violence in an effort to exorcise spirits they were thought to possess (Munyi, 2012). Later in the nineteenth century, the eugenics movement treated them as genetically undesirable leading to their isolation, sterilization and death (Black, 2012). These ideas are inextricably intertwined and a result of the creation of the "norm." "The word 'Normal' as 'constituting, conforming to, not deviating or different from, the common type or standard, regular, usual' only enters the English language around 1840" (Davis 1997, p. 10). However, as Dolmage (2014) points out, notions regarding the "ideal" that resulted in a "normative mandate . . . [and] normative processes" (p. 23) existed well before this time.

In terms of education, the development of the norm coincides directly with the idea of grades organized around age, marks, a set curricula and the development of special education (Woodill 1992, p. 7). Invoking the work of Foucault, Toohey (2000) asserts that beginning in the 17th and 18th century, "practices of categorizing individuals and attaching them to their identities were enacted in particular institutions (like prisons and schools) . . . individuals then, were constructed by the practices of the institutions with which they were engaged" (p. 9). Norm-referenced understandings of the "ideal" have created divisions and hierarchies that construct those who do not mirror norms as deficient and Other than normal. Such hierarchies "enable the articulation of standards so that people can be compared and differentiated on the basis of their relation to standards" (Toohey, 2000, p. 8). The articulation of norms and modes of comparison has also meant "individuals categorized as too far from a norm [would] undergo sanctions to 'normalise' them" (Foucault, 1979, in Toohey, 2000, p. 9). The creation and mass application of the norm consequently furthered a "hegemony of normalcy" (Davis, 1997, p. 26). Davis argues that the entire "social process of disabling arrived with industrialization and with a set of practices and discourses that are linked to late eighteenth- and nineteenth-century notions of nationality, race, gender, criminality, sexual orientation, and so on" (pp. 9–10). Binary ways of understanding the world were manifest through this set of practices and discourses. These divisions can be understood as a by-product of connections between the development of statistical science, the creation of numerical representations of normalcy, and the eugenics movement. The invention of IQ, "one of the most popular and controversial concepts in the history of psychology" (Gregory, 2004, p. 14) as measured by the Stanford-Binet published in 1916 and the subsequent psychological testing movement are clear examples of hegemonic practices and processes that have cemented dominant and problematic notions about what is considered to be normal or abnormal and thus, have furthered the able/disabled divide.

Davis (1997) reminds us that "almost all the early statisticians had one thing in common: they were eugenicists" (p. 14). The field of "statistics is bound up with eugenics because the central insight of statistics is the idea that a population can be normed" (p. 14). Society has been seduced by these scientific constructions of normalcy despite the fact that "the invaluable rule of statistics is that phenomenon will always conform to a bell curve. So " 'norming the non-norm' is an activity as problematic as untying the Gordian knot" (p. 14). Therefore, "the problem is the way that normalcy is constructed to create "the problem" (p. 9). In its misguided belief in and commitment to the norm, society ultimately creates and constructs deficit when norms are not met. McLaren (1990) describes this process as it existed within schools:

> The "feeble-minded" were in effect "created" as a category at the turn of the century when education was made free and compulsory. There had, of course, been some members of society who because of their mental or physical handicaps had been perceived by their neighbors as somehow deficient. With the emergence of a modern, centralized, mass form of education, however, one entered a new world. To an unprecedented extent enormous numbers of children were subjected to common tests, examinations, and medical inspections. Those who met the new norms were declared "normal"; those who did not were labeled as inadequate. (p. 91)

The pursuit of statistical measurements of human normalcy has deceptively communicated that such measurement gathering somehow "helps to improve humans so that deviations from the norm diminish" (p. 14). These understandings have been associated with "positive eugenics" (Black, 2003) and have been instrumental in creating and then marginalizing those constructed as Other in relation to the norm. Such constructions have fallen along racial lines as many of "the IQ tests to which students were subjected naturally relied on cultural experiences and the verbal skills and practices of the cultural elite" (Law Reform Commission of Canada, 1980 in McLaren, 1990, p. 92). Belenky, Bond, and Weinstock (1997) further explore this deficit understanding of Otherness. They describe the typically subordinate positions marginalized groups occupy within society as Other. These positions are understood by dominant groups to be the result of not being "endowed with intellectual power" (p. 8). Such presumptions adhere to and reinforce norm/ non-norm, us/other classification.

> Because dualisms seem to bring great clarity to the most ambiguous and elusive issues, people are particularly apt to use them to organize their thinking about morality, epistemology, and identity development—clearly among the most difficult and the most important subjects ordinary human beings try to ponder. (p. 20)

These polarities further the norm/Other divide and foster hierarchies, which distort social relationships as they satiate perverse needs for certainty and conformity. Since statistically speaking, the Other can never be "improved" toward the norm, understandings of normalcy rather than enhancing humanity have rationalized the marginalization and destruction of those constructed as Other. As such, connections between statistics and eugenics have been instrumental in furthering xenophobic as well as holocaustic and genocidal orientations (Davis, 1997).

Dominant discourses and practices that shape education have been heavily informed by understandings of and investments in statistical constructions of normalcy. The dominant disability discourse of the twentieth century that prevails in education is heavily informed by medical models and metaphors that view and position people with disabilities as patients with ailments in need of diagnosing, pathologizing, and normalizing (Heydon & Iannacci, 2008). This essentialist model (Hosking, 2008) is a re-tooling of previous ideas informed by eugenics as it continues to configure disability as an innate flaw within a person that requires interventions to "fix," Baker (2002) makes explicit the impact eugenics discourse has had on education. "From the outset eugenicists had direct things to say to schools and . . . this aspect of eugenic thought has proved to be more pervasive and more enduring than the more spectacular arguments around sterilization" (Lowe, 1997, in Baker, 2002, p. 665). Lowe (1997) specifically identifies how several areas of educational policy and practice such as testing, differential treatment of minorities, the questioning of both hereditary and environmental factors in the quality of students' home life and mothering, and the transmission of opinions through children's books and school texts are deeply influenced by eugenic ideas (in Baker, 2002, p. 671). Iannacci (2005) demonstrates how eugenic discourse is manifest in the ways in which children in his study were assessed, the literacy instruction made available to them, the ways their home lives were depicted, and finally in the inadequate number of culturally relevant resources provided for them. Further the various evaluation tools or "perfecting technologies" (p. 675) that were used in schools to "hunt for disability" also indicated the continued influence of eugenics within education. Relatedly, Baker states that "The new eugenics is concerned with perfecting technologies to secure quality citizenship through the homogenization of racial/national populations at some level" (Baker, 2002, p. 676) and astutely notes, that "In the often well-intended hunt for disability . . . disability becomes reinscribed as an "outlaw ontology" (Wrigley, 1996 in Baker, 2002, p. 665), reinvesting eugenic discourse in a new language that maintains an "ableist normativity" (Campbell, 2000 in Baker, 2002, p. 665). This "outlaw ontology" is defined as a "deep-seated despise of unevenness, asymmetry, or imbalance that places bodies-minds labeled as disabled at the edge of the abyss, pushing the limits of human subjectivity" (Campbell, 2000 in Baker, 2002, p. 674). Hosking (2008), for example, points out that disability has been conceived "as personal misfortune preferably to be prevented and definitely to be cured, privileges 'normalcy' over the 'abnormal,' presumes able-bodied norms are inevitable, and values economic productivity as an essential aspect of personhood" (p. 6).

## INCLUSION CONFUSION

Although we are now in an era of unprecedented litigiousness that has to some degree lessened human rights abuses experienced by people with disabilities, the nature of disability and how we collectively respond to people with disabilities within institutions remains conceptually unclear and operationally problematic. Inclusion, like disability, has been and continues to be a ubiquitous and often misunderstood term within the field of education despite its dominant presence[2]. Roth (2015) uses the term "inclusion confusion" to name this lack of clarity. Hibbert (2013) astutely captures one of the most significant issues with respect to inclusion.

. . . during my professional practice in a school system, we initiated the under-theorized move in the Special Education field toward "inclusive classrooms"; a practice that saw "exceptional" students served within their own classrooms rather than being withdrawn or assigned full-time to segregated placements. The superficial and problematic "shift" occurred in the physical world; it was only a matter of moving bodies, scheduling resources, and collaborating with classroom teachers. The necessary and complex epistemological shift has proven much more challenging . . . To move from a universal approach to practice that focuses on optics, to a differentiated response designed around students' needs, abilities, and resources, requires a sophisticated shift in thinking. (p. 29)

My experiences, concerns, and perspectives mirror those shared by Hibbert (2013) and require further exploration and critical analysis in order to clarify some of the problematic misnomers currently shaping how inclusion is conceptualized and operationalized within education and the ways in which this has adversely affected people with disabilities.

The following narratives are constructed from firsthand experiences, teaching, working with teachers and teacher candidates, research, observations in schools and stories shared by various colleagues, parents and students with whom I have had the privilege of working. The narratives are therefore methodologically composed from multiple field texts based on various experiences (Clandinin et al., 2010). Their coalesced composition "allows for multiple inquiries across multiple times, places, and projects . . . " (p. 85). These composed texts that draw on experiences I have had in education over the past 25 years are provided as a way to "stay awake to complex stories and, through inquiry into the tensions shaped in the living and telling of these stories, to imagine new possibilities because of the educative potential and tensions" (p. 85). As each of the stories is an amalgam, they are not simply anecdotal and idiosyncratic but rather representative of many specific similar stories. I have used these stories with educators in professional development contexts, in my teaching and while giving academic talks. During these instances, several educators have told me they have had exactly the same experience or were certain that the story was about their student/child, class, school, school board and so forth. Any resonance that occurs as a result of these stories is meant to enable the process of reconceptualization that is pursued throughout this book. This process is aided by the analysis that will occur after these narratives have been shared.

## STACEY'S CHAIR AND TABLE

At the very back of the classroom there is a table pressed against the wall. Two chairs are placed at it. The chairs at the table are permanently reserved for Stacey and the educational assistant assigned to her. Stacey is a smiley, demonstrative child who takes great pleasure in sounds and visuals and is animated when listening to and looking at a variety of auditory and visual texts. Stacey, a student identified with multiple exceptionalities has severe physical and cognitive challenges that stem from birth. Her chair is equipped in ways that enable her to sit upright and the educational assistant lifts her into and out of this chair when she is in need of using the bathroom or during transitions. Stacey and her educational assistant sit at this table all day. Her educational assistant sets up a tape recorder and various audio tapes that contain sounds and music for Stacey to listen to. She also shares a variety of photos and pictures with Stacey and names and points to things on them. Although Stacey is officially considered non-verbal, her reactions to these texts are expressive and communicate joy, wonder, and engagement. When she does not like the music/sounds or pictures the educational assistant provides, Stacey is equally communicative about her displeasure. While she is at the table with her EA, the rest of the students in Stacey's class and the teacher proceed without her.

Today the teacher shares the short film adaptation of *The Snowman* by Raymond Briggs. She invites the class to the carpet to gather around the television, sits beside it, and explains that she will be holding up the picture book version of the story as the film proceeds and as the story unfolds. Although the picture book is highly visual and contains no words and the film adaptation contains beautiful music and animation, Stacey and her EA do not join the class to watch and hear the story and film despite the fact this is exactly the type of experience Stacey enjoys. Such behavior is the norm within this classroom and the teacher believes it necessary in order that Stacey not "distract" the other students. Stacey's educational assistant and those who fill in for her when she is away find this disconcerting and have discussed it among themselves, but never with the teacher since they believe it is not their place to do so. Stacey's educational assistant is frequently absent as she finds it difficult to lift her and often has back pain as a result.

Stacey's school used to have a room that contained specialized equipment that included lifts and auditory and pictorial sensory boards among other materials that students like Stacey would use and benefit from. At one point students with special needs could access this room throughout the day whenever they needed it. At other times in the day, they were part of a larger regular class assigned to them based on their age. However, a few years prior to Stacey arriving at the school, it was decided that this specialized classroom did not reflect inclusion and so, the contents of the room were removed and the space was converted into a regular classroom, the very one Stacey was placed in on the grounds that withdrawal is not inclusive.

## MOVING ON AND THEN?

The special education resource classroom teacher is told that one of her students is moving. Lance will attend a school in the same board of education but part of a different family of schools. Lance is inquisitive, highly social, and very conscientious of his appearance. His hair is especially important to him and is always styled with care. In fact, Lance has said repeatedly that he wants to be a hair dresser. His special education resource teacher thought that she would be teaching Lance for another year after the current one and would eventually transition Lance to a nearby vocational school that has an excellent cosmetology program that includes an authentic functioning hair salon with regular paying clients.

Lance has been diagnosed officially with a mild intellectual disability and struggles a great deal with math and literacy expectations for his grade. His special education resource classroom teacher provides him with necessary modified and accommodated math and literacy instruction. This has made a significant difference to Lance's self-esteem. Throughout his elementary school experiences, he has had varying levels of support. When literacy and numeracy instruction became too difficult, Lance would shut down completely and articulated to both peers and teachers that he is a "retard" and can't do the work. This behavior has not occurred since Lance was placed in the special education class and further, Lance's literacy and numeracy skills have developed more so than ever before. Lance attends the special education class for approximately half of the day and has lunch and the remainder of the school day in his "age appropriate" grade. His general education classroom teacher and the special education resource classroom teacher meet frequently to discuss accommodations and modifications that Lance requires. His special education classroom teacher has created literacy and numeracy programming for Lance that is relevant and linked to his goal of becoming a hair dresser. He is especially engaged and active during this individualized programming and instruction.

As Lance is moving, his special education classroom teacher calls his new school and speaks to the special education teacher there in order to prepare for the transition. During the phone conversation, the special education teacher at Lance's new school asks how many minutes of support Lance receives during the day. Immediately after explaining that Lance is in a self-contained class for half the school day, the special education teacher at Lance's new school states that the school does not believe in that model of support because it is an "inclusion" school. Lance will be placed in a regular classroom all day with some occasional support and monitoring from the special education teacher within that classroom. When Lance's challenges, needs, and interests and the subsequent type of literacy and numeracy programming that has been created for him are raised, the special education teacher at Lance's new school quickly reiterates that the school opposes any withdrawal under the guise of inclusion.

## AT THE BOARD OFFICE

For many years, teacher candidates completing their initial teacher certification individually tutor students who struggle with literacy in schools as part of the program in which they are enrolled. They create literacy instruction based on individual needs, assets, and interests and tutor students in a quiet area that allows them to access a variety of instructional strategies that may be auditory, visual, tactile, and kinesthetic in nature depending on student preferences and strengths. The tutored students are nominated by their school for the program and parents sign permission forms that allow the student to participate. Any student who is averse to the program does not have to participate. The program has received positive feedback for many years from parents, children, teachers, and teacher candidates.

When a new superintendent in charge of programming is hired at the board office level, becomes aware of and concerned about the inclusivity of the program, she immediately sends an email to all teachers indicating that students must be tutored by teacher candidates within their classrooms since doing otherwise does not reflect inclusion. The university tutoring placement coordinator becomes aware of this email when teacher candidates who have been tutoring in quiet areas in schools are faced with having to tutor in classrooms, making sessions difficult and ineffective.

A meeting is arranged at the board office to discuss the matter. The university tutoring placement coordinator enters a room filled with many board officials including the program superintendent who sent out the email. This superintendent begins the meeting by stating that the tutoring program does not align with inclusion since students are withdrawn from their classrooms to attend the tutoring sessions. The university coordinator explains that the program runs over the course of a few months, is designed specifically to address the literacy needs of students who have difficulty with literacy, and that the one-on-one instruction designed for students by teacher candidates requires spaces that allow the students and the teacher candidates to participate in activity that they would be unable to in the confines of the regular classroom. The university tutoring placement coordinator notes that this one-on-one instruction is especially helpful as the number of special education teachers and services in the board has been recently significantly reduced. The coordinator also points out that, as a result of the tutoring, students' overall achievement in their regular classrooms has demonstrated improvement.

The school board equity officer attending the meeting raises concerns about the definition of inclusion used by the superintendent of programs to validate the decision about the location of the tutoring. He re-frames the tutoring as an equity issue since those students who receive the tutoring require a level of sustained and focused support that the schools cannot offer due to limited and dwindling resources. As a compromise, the superintendent sends another email to all teachers in the board with students who participate in the tutoring program stating that if tutoring in the classroom is not working, teacher candidates and students may once again hold tutoring sessions outside of the classroom. A week later all teacher candidates report that they are again tutoring outside of the classrooms and that sessions are going well.

## ONE MORE THING

A group of educators are about to begin some professional development regarding inclusion during a summer course. Most are there because they want to improve their practice, some because they require the credential and a couple because they were told by an administrator that they had to attend. The instructor begins by asking them to form groups and to discuss and record what they know about and what their experiences have been with inclusion, including challenges they have had in enacting it. The instructor visits groups and listens to the discussions. One of the teachers is clearly agitated. The instructor notices and has a brief conversation with him which begins by asking how he is. The teacher sharply tells the instructor that his administrator "forced" him to attend the class and that he is frustrated by his professional life, all of the "fads" in education like inclusion, and would prefer to be left alone and not participate in the course. The instructor is sympathetic and acknowledges how frustrated he is with all of the "fads" in education, but then clearly explains to him that inclusion is not a fad and that the course will begin by exploring inclusion as a legal obligation within education and enable participants in the course to critically examine their boards, schools, and classrooms in ways that forward inclusion. The instructor invites the teacher to give the course a chance and to remain open to using it to address his professional frustrations, and as such to make it as useful as possible. The teacher is surprised to hear that inclusion is legally required and tentatively agrees to the instructor's invitation.

Throughout the course the teacher's level of engagement increases as his frustration fades. He uses class activities, discussions and assignments to critically explore his practice in relation to supporting students with special needs. He is honest about his difficulties. His colleagues offer support, strategies, advice, narratives, and are equally honest about their own challenges. He begins his final assignment with a reconstruction of his initial discussion with the instructor and admits that he was not aware of his legal obligations with respect to inclusion. He also shares that prior to taking the class, he had contemplated leaving teaching altogether. The remainder of the assignment critically explores his classroom practice using readings, activities, discussions, and presentations experienced throughout the course to reflect on and identify specific and concrete ways to revise his practice. In the final paragraph of the assignment he states that he is once again committed to his teaching and his students, articulates that he is feeling professionally renewed and looking forward to rather than dreading the upcoming school year.

## IT'S TIME

Vlad was withdrawn from his grade eight classroom daily to receive support with literacy and math from a special education resource teacher. He was identified as having a learning disability in the second grade and had been receiving consistent special education withdrawal support from this teacher since then. The special education teacher knew Vlad very well and designed instruction for him that appealed to his interests (e.g., structures, robotics) throughout their time together. Now in grade eight, both Vlad and the special education teacher noted how well he was doing in math, a subject in which he also demonstrated a great deal of interest. Mathematics programming and instruction provided by Vlad's special education teacher was no longer modified (below grade level expectations), but he continued to need instructional and assessment accommodations particularly when the content was language heavy. Although Vlad's placement review meeting wasn't until May, the special education teacher decided to discuss the matter of math instruction with Vlad's regular grade eight classroom teacher who was both open and demonstratively apt at accommodating and engaging learners with disabilities in a variety of curriculum areas. During the meeting, the regular grade eight teacher was both enthusiastic and agreeable to having Vlad transition to attending the math class. Vlad's parents were told about the potential change and asked if they agreed and they did. Vlad was told about the change and also agreed. The following Monday, he received special education support for literacy but remained in his regular classroom for every other subject including math. Vlad's performance and disposition were monitored to ensure the appropriate decision had been made, and he was occasionally asked how he felt coping with the change. During his placement review meeting in May, Vlad's special education and regular classroom teacher reported on his success with the change of placement in math.

## DISCUSSION

The previous narratives demonstrate the need to explore and clarify some of the legalities of inclusion given contradictory ideas that circulate about its status and form within education. On the one hand, educators at various stages of their careers working in a variety of contexts (classrooms, school boards, universities, etc.) can conflate inclusion with the myriad of trends, initiatives, and mandates that have come and gone throughout their careers. The ways in which these fads and directives have disappeared only to be replaced by other policies, programs, pedagogies, and practices has created a culture of skepticism about the longevity of any practice including inclusion and misunderstandings about educators' responsibilities in ensuring its implementation. This has also resulted in what Burm (2016) identifies as policy and compassion fatigue among educators. To this end it is crucial to point out that inclusion is law rather than yet another fleeting trend/movement in education. Various national and provincial laws, policies, and bills (e.g., the Canadian Charter of Rights and Freedoms, the Ontario Human Rights Code, The Education Act) create a legal hierarchy that guarantees and requires exceptional students to have access to public education. Parts of the Education Act make explicit that all school boards are to provide special education programs and services for all students regardless of exceptionality. Similar laws that mandate inclusion are in place throughout the United States and United Kingdom. Canadian, US, and UK laws, policies, and bills are further internationally supported by The UN Convention on the Rights of Persons with Disabilities, which asserts that everyone has the right to an inclusive education. Importantly, Canada was among the first countries to sign the convention and continues to be accountable to its overarching principles. As such there shouldn't be any confusion about the nature of inclusion in terms of its positioning. It quite simply is required by law.

Contradictorily, a superficial accountability to inclusion as evidenced in the narratives, has meant that inclusion within education is most often taken to mean the practice of including students with disabilities in regular school classes. This optics driven and problematic misunderstanding of inclusion is pervasive and perplexing. To be clear, there is no legal/policy language to support or validate this model. Inclusion is not, nor should it ever be, understood as a geographic location in a school (e.g., the "regular" classroom) and as such this way of understanding/enacting inclusion does not legally adhere to inclusion/inclusive practice. Specht (2016) points out that "The misconception a lot of times is that if we just put kids with disabilities in the classroom, that's inclusion. Inclusion is based on the principle of equity, justice, and the understanding that all kids belong" (Bouevitch, 2016). Geographically placing students in a regular classroom all day or allowing them to use a resource room does not therefore ensure inclusion. Situations such as those documented in *Stacey's Chair and Table* where students are placed in regular classrooms all day under the guise of inclusion and never included as a member of that learning community, are not acceptable or indicative of inclusion. Inclusion does not require that every student with a disability be placed in the regular classroom all day. Such an understanding is reminiscent of integration or mainstreaming, a model that was unsuccessful in responding to the needs, assets, and interests of all students. Instead inclusion means offering a range of placement options if the model is to be forwarded in ways that are responsive to students. Winzer (2008) clarifies the two models and the central issues they raise. "Integration and mainstreaming sought to change individuals to fit the existing system; inclusion seeks to change the system so that exclusion and marginalization are avoided" (p. 43). What's vital to inclusion and repeated frequently in legal/policy language that mandates it is the importance of having students' needs met. To that end, education and educators are to provide students who have a disability the least restrictive environment possible, which means ensuring that placement options available are safe, engaging, responsive to their needs, and do not academically, socially, psychologically, emotionally, etc., marginalize students who have a disability. This means that placement options are idiosyncratic rather than universal and decided upon based on the needs, best interests, and assets of the students. When placement decisions are made using this information, they are reflective of an ethical praxis. Interestingly, this clarification and validation of decision making needs to occur despite the fact that placement options identified during Identification Placement Review Committee (IPRC) processes and listed on Individual Educational Plans (IEPs) (legal processes and documents in Ontario but similarly present throughout North America and the UK) are very clear and as follows:

- Regular class with indirect support
- Special education class with partial integration
- Regular class with resource assistance
- Regular class with withdrawal assistance
- Special education class full-time

There are still many full-time, self-contained special education classrooms in schools that better meet the needs of some students who have a disability. All placement options need to be thoughtfully and responsively decided based on what the student requires and where he/she will thrive, and must be fully agreed upon by parents/guardians. These placement options are not fixed. They are to be reviewed whenever there is need to do so, not merely when required by a bureaucratic calendar, as was demonstrated in the case of the *It's Time* narrative. This is equally true when students in general education classrooms are having difficulties.

⌊Providing placement support for students that is responsive to their needs as well as developing an individual educational plan for them if needed is a duty of care issue that does not require a process to authorize or an institutional identification (e.g., learning disabled). It is ethically and legally imperative that we understand inclusion to be dependent upon a school's ability to develop provisions for students and that these provisions are flexible, fluid, and temporary. As such, not every student who is provided placement support or an IEP can or will need to be formally identified as having a disability. In fact, our ability to respond to students' needs can often prevent this from ever happening. In short, when changes are noted regarding a student's needs, so too should placement possibilities. This is what needs to govern decisions for students as opposed to a bureaucratically organized, superficial and fossilized adherence to inclusion.⌋ Doing so does not mean a dismantling of special education and the formal identification processes it uses, as students can benefit from what it may offer them when needed. Rather, what is required is a commitment to deconstructing and reconceptualizing what education and therefore special education are and do in order to fulfill its ethical obligation to respect diversity and respond to it by creating inclusive learning environments for all students. This specifically means making decisions for/with students in ways that are responsive to them rather than restricted by bureaucracy as demonstrated in the *It's Time* narrative. This is also pragmatic given the fact that resources and special education funding are limited. Although we may be hunting for disability more and more within schools, we are less and less able to financially support this hunt as it is both expensive and resource heavy. There are both ethical and financial reasons why we need to critically rethink pathologizing processes that treat resources as infinite while using them inefficiently.

My experiences have consistently verified the *potential* effectiveness of various placement options in forwarding inclusion within schools. The word *potential* is key. What needs to be highlighted from the *Moving On and Then?* narrative is that programming and instruction provided by Lance's special education teacher was pedagogically sound, engaging and responsive to his needs, interests and assets. Similarly, in the *It's Time* narrative, both Vlad's special education teacher and regular classroom teacher demonstrated that they were *both* able to provide Vlad with effective and generative learning opportunities that were dynamic and focused on Vlad's development rather than on fragmented drill and kill instruction based on his perceived deficiencies, an essentialized identity as a "student with a disability" and an adherence to official processes that prescribe when program decisions can be made, as opposed to when they should be made. Hehir (2002) argues that we need to "move away from the current obsession with placement toward an obsession with results" (p. 25). As such, all placement decisions and programming (self-contained, withdrawal, in-class support, etc.) should be contingent on the student's success, not on system defaults and therefore designed in ways that demonstrate exemplary teaching and collegial communication.

There are other dominant notions regarding inclusion and students with disabilities that the narratives demonstrate that also require critical analysis. First, the idea that students with disabilities are a hindrance to "normal" students is inaccurate, problematic, and limited/limiting. This unfortunately continues to be reinforced in schools as demonstrated in the *Stacey's Chair and Table* narrative, and inadvertently, in educational research. A year-long study conducted by Dessemontet & Bless (2013), for example, actually  focused on the impact including children with disabilities in general education classrooms had on their peers. Although the study demonstrated that children with disabilities do not have a negative impact on the academic achievement of their peers who do not have a disability, the focus and scope of the research is telling, troubling, and in need of interrogation. The idea that the only thing that is important is whether "normal" students in classrooms are not negatively affected by their peers who have a disability unquestionably reinforces ableism within the classroom, and thus has a negative impact on all students within that classroom. This question of "negative impact" furthers the idea that what matters is the protection of normal students from that of their disabled peers as opposed to furthering genuine understanding of disabilities/people with disabilities in ways that advance students' education and ultimately, their humanity. Again, what needs to be explored are asset-oriented ways (Heydon & Iannacci, 2008) of seeing disability and what students with disabilities bring to learning communities rather than being positioned and researched as potential liabilities.

This point is also made when we consider Fraser & Shields's (2010, p.15) exploration of how students with disabilities have been "treated as ghosts (virtually ignored), guests (respected but not integrated), or pets (cosseted and pampered) in the classroom" (in Meyer & Bevan-Brown, 2005). Without question, Stacey's positioning within the classroom was that of a ghost. Although this is perhaps the most insidious classroom identity ascribed to a student with a disability, guests and pets are equally miseducative and *do* negatively impact both students with special needs and their non-disabled peers. Further and most importantly, the ghost, guest, pet positioning/approach to inclusion is entirely violative for students with special needs and demonstrates how their presence is merely symbolic, and that their needs, interests, and who they are is irrelevant. Alternatively, seeing them as members of a learning community who have specific needs that require addressing is educative and fosters a genuine understanding of people with disabilities. Doing otherwise is reminiscent of disability erasure fueled by the pretense that ignoring someone's disability and placing them in a regular classroom (despite their invisibility in that classroom) is an appropriate response. Further, these particular miseducative ways of being also position people with disabilities as pawns of inclusion as they are placed in regular classrooms and ignored, infantilized or tolerated in the name of satiating a misinformed and troubling understanding of/response to inclusion that rids education/educators of responsibility for creating authentic learning environments for students with disabilities where they are engaged, supported, understood, valued, and enabled to demonstrate their ways of knowing.

## RESEARCHER/RESEARCH INTERSECTIONS

Having personally had poor experiences while being withdrawn for special education support as a child, one would think that I would not be advocating for any placement other than the regular classroom. What needs to be understood is that impoverished pedagogy (Iannacci, 2018) during withdrawal special education support or in self-contained special education classrooms *is* the issue, *not* the model of support. This issue has been exacerbated by the special education field and its dominant forms of instruction offered during what has been termed "interventions." These are synthetic, scope and sequenced, context-reduced (Cummins, 2005), fragment-focused forms of pedagogy believed to be necessary for students with disabilities as they are understood as unable to manage any other form of instruction. Once again a deficit understanding of disability not only essentializes the student, but the form of instruction they are provided. Deficit-focused pedagogies are inextricably linked to ascribed deficit identities assigned to students with special needs. In short, what we think/understand about students with disabilities, how we talk about them and what we do for them are inextricably linked. When disability is understood as a deficit and language used to describe students with disabilities is deficit-oriented and focused on pathologies, forms of instruction are viewed from and shaped by medical model perspectives ensuring impoverished and disabling pedagogies devoid of utility and engagement.

In chapter four, the issue of pedagogy is examined further and examples of meaningful, purposeful, and engaging instruction are provided.

This chapter has attempted to critically explore deeply flawed notions regarding disability and inclusion in order to problematize limited conceptualizations and misunderstandings that have confined and restricted people with disabilities and our responses to them within education. Further, the chapter destabilized dominant grand narratives that have prevented a dynamic and complex understanding and operationalizing of inclusion. This exploration is intended to provide educators with information to allow them to re-think what they have come to know/understand about disability and inclusion and how to lead in ways that are responsive and dynamic. The chapter therefore provides a preliminary frame for critically thinking about inclusion/ inclusive practices in order to be responsive to a complex, asset-oriented understanding of disability and the various needs and resources students with disabilities have. The next chapter further explores these assets, resources, and needs by focusing on disability as philosophy and epistemology and on identifying principles and understandings that foster necessary shifts in how disability is spoken of, thought of, and responded to within education. The chapter explores disability as a way of knowing and an identity in order to demonstrate a marked difference from current discourses that position it as innate defectiveness.

## NOTES

1. See Dolmage (2014) for an extensive exploration of these myths that include the "disability as pathology and disability as a sign from the above" myths (pp. 34–37).

2. Inclusion within education also applies to cultural, linguistic, racial, religious, gender, sexual, socio-economic, etc., diversity and the ways in which it has been responded to within school contexts. This chapter and book, however, focuses on inclusion as it relates to students with disabilities within education.

# Chapter Three

# Disability: Philosophical and Epistemological Perspectives

> . . . let's pretend that public schooling is not concerned purely with literacy, math, and that nebulous thing called academic achievement and that its arbitrary focus is in fact physical education. Let's extend the reversal and imagine that PE [physical education] is *the* thing, the knowledge-performance that matters to how I judge you, who you can be, and what you can have. How fast *can* you run, move, slide, or roll? If I beat you, does that make you a problem? Or is the problem the notion of beating, of winning and losing, of faster and slower, of normal and abnormal in the face of rhetoric claiming respect for human diversity?
>
> —Bernadette Baker, 2002, p. 698

Although discourses, language, laws, and processes that govern disability must be critically examined, forwarding an asset-oriented (Heydon & Iannacci, 2008), responsive model of inclusion requires a grander conversation. The "bigger picture" of inclusion requires that we embrace and are genuinely responsive to the diversity people possess and bring with them into public institutions. For schools this specifically means building welcoming communities where all students are valued, provided for, have a sense of belonging, and are actively engaged in their education. Again, this philosophy does not necessarily exclude the possibility of special education classes—inclusion can be accomplished through a variety of placement options and participation in co-curricular activities, social events, programs, and so forth. However, inclusion goes well beyond legal requirements and thoughtful considerations regarding placement options. Importantly, inclusion requires asset-oriented beliefs and attitudes about the various ways people live in and know the world as well as how they express and demonstrate their understanding of it. Kunc (1992) provides insights that forward philosophical understandings about inclusion:

> The fundamental principle of inclusive education is the valuing of diversity within the human community. . . .When inclusive education is fully embraced, we abandon the idea that children have to become "normal" in order to contribute to the world. . . . We begin to look beyond typical ways of becoming valued members of the community, and in doing so, begin to realize the achievable goal of providing all children with an authentic sense of belonging. (pp. 38–39)

A central concern of inclusion therefore is being critically aware of the tyranny of the norm and working to destabilize its coercive power. This requires that educators see present systems that categorize, organize and evaluate people based on their age, stage and in relation to norms as problematic and deeply flawed. Developmental and standardized understandings of learning and knowledge therefore are questioned as are notions of what human beings are supposed to know and do based on spans of time (e.g., "By the end of grade___, students will:", "By the end of this course, students will:"[1]). Learning, development, and knowledge are understood as being shaped by a variety of factors and reflective of an array of human variance rather than *things* that can be measured against established norms and subsequently understood as less than, deficient, and in need of fixing. Harman (2009) captures how essential this thinking is to inclusion:

> Successful models of inclusion believe that ALL children are different, and ALL children can learn. There is nothing about a child that needs to be "fixed" in order for that child to fit into a system. The school system, as a whole, is enabled to change in order to meet the individual needs of ALL learners. (Harman, 2009, p. 1, original emphasis)

In order for this model of inclusion to exist, we need to understand disability as diversity and identity rather than as deficiency. This requires that we see students as possessing a variety of social, cognitive, artistic, emotional, cultural, linguistic, and affective assets that must be recognized and addressed. When a student has a disability, it is understood as part of who the student is, how they understand the world and one of the many legacies (Delpit, 2003) he/she has that are valued and valuable to the community to which the student belongs. This community sees the various identities of its members as inherently educative, worthy of celebrating and reciprocally learning from. The community's primary focus is not on assimilating any of its members toward a single way of being, seeing, understanding, acting, or knowing but rather collectively benefitting from the myriad of experiences and epistemologies present within that community. This is a stance that inherently works to combat ableist attitudes focused on norming the "abnormal."

As stated in the previous chapter, what we think and understand about students with disabilities, how we talk about them and what we do for/with them are inextricably linked. As such, an educator's epistemology is directly related to their ability to see, capitalize on, and forward students' epistemologies and identities. Interestingly, notions of disability as diversity (Kim & Aquino, 2017) that draw on rich theoretical perspectives present in culturally responsive pedagogy are beginning to merge to form "culturally relevant disability pedagogy" (Yuknis & Bernstein, 2017, p. 4). This new framework seeks to disrupt the deficit narrative assigned to disability and "bring together theory and practice to support the success of students with various disabilities in the higher education classroom" (p. 16). Although this is helpful work, these perspectives need to be applied to students with disabilities in elementary school contexts as well. This is especially important as children are already cast as inferior and unfinished "others" in relation to adults and adult centric notions of what is normal, valuable, and therefore necessary to do to children to ensure their civility and productivity. Children with disabilities are additionally "Othered among Others" (Iannacci, 2005) as their disabilities further cast them as incapable, abnormal, and in need of intervention. These relations of power and the importance of recognizing, responding to, and reciprocally learning from the epistemological diversity that is available to community members in inclusive environments within schools is demonstrated in the following narrative and subsequent discussion and analysis.

## EVAN'S PAPER CRANE

Mr. Green was in his second year of teaching but was experiencing many firsts. It was his first grade four class and the first time he would be teaching a student identified as having a mild intellectual disability (MID). The student's name was Evan and the special education teacher who had been working with him since he was in grade one provided little information about him other than his official MID identification, that he was that he was "very delayed" and that she enjoyed working with him.

Mr. Green was anxious about having Evan in his class. He had immersed himself in the grade four curriculum during the summer and was overwhelmed by the amount of content he was required to cover. He was also anxious because he had been provided almost no information about teaching students with disabilities during his Bachelor of Education and had no previous experience working with them. Curious as to what an MID was, he looked at the official definition provided by the Ministry of Education. This further exasperated his anxieties as it characterized MID as a "disorder," "an inability," "below average intelligence," "slow intellectual development," and suggested that MID students required "considerable support and modifications" by the teacher. Wanting desperately to be able to support Evan, Mr. Green sought out advice from his former teachers. This too further fueled his concerns. Statements like, "very behind in all areas," "don't expect much," "give him easy things to do," "he's practically silent, not a problem," "mischievous at times," and "don't worry about him, he's getting support from the special education teacher" did nothing to give Mr. Green a sense of how to engage with Evan.

During the first week of school, Mr. Green looked through the duo-tang of photocopied sheets the special education teacher provided for Evan during their 45 minute a day sessions. These black line masters were fill-in-the-blanks phonics tasks and brief paragraphs followed by questions that could be answered in one or two words. Despite this, Evan and the special education teacher seemed to have a warm relationship. Evan clearly liked spending time with her. Some days the only smile Evan produced was when he left the classroom to see her.

Frustrated, Mr. Green pulled Evan's student record from the front office to see what he could find out about how to teach him. Results on official standardized tests showed that Evan was nowhere near meeting grade four expectations and standards. Report card after report card said the same thing. "Doesn't participate, extremely quiet and withdrawn, has difficulty reading and writing, not meeting grade level expectations, occasional behavior issues." Mr. Green wondered how Evan's parents could have allowed things to get so bad. Why weren't they doing more? Did they care? Were they capable? Was there something wrong with them too? Whatever the case, it was clear to him that they would be of no help to him.

Evan's educational psychological assessment described in detail his deficiencies and identified his official designation of Mild Intellectual Disability. The four bullet points at the end of the report that described "instructional needs" were as follows:

- separate larger tasks into smaller ones
- provide extra time to complete tasks
- provide one-on-one support
- modify expectations

These points provided nothing in the way of information that would help Mr. Green teach Evan and quell his anxieties about how to do so.

Mr. Green consulted a "special education" textbook he found on the two shelves marked "faculty resource library" in the staff room and read the chapter on MID. It reiterated the same things that were present in the Ministry of Education definition and described the problematic nature of having a MID in terms of learning and socialization. The specifics it did provide were completely focused on naming the myriad deficiencies of students with MID and the biological causes of MID. Again, Mr. Green was bombarded by words and phrases such as inability, socially inappropriate, immature, diminished, low self-esteem, difficulty, lacking, poor interpersonal skills, deficits, limitations, weak, inefficient, impaired, delayed, limited, failure, disordered, learned helplessness, errors, lack of skills, does not, cannot, reliant, problem. Mr. Green was perplexed when he reached the last page of the chapter and had not encountered a single piece of information that would help him teach Evan. He reached for another special education focused text, and another and yet another until there weren't any left. All of the texts said the same things in the same way and used the same language. Mr. Green gained no further insights about MID and Evan other than to expect problems.

As the school year began, everything that Mr. Green had been told by his colleagues, the student record, assessments, reports, and experts was what he began to see. Evan was disengaged, nearly silent all of the time, occasionally behaved immaturely, and incapable of most of the tasks Mr. Green assigned and progressively became both sadder and visibly frustrated. Although larger tasks were broken down into smaller ones for Evan, he completed very few of even the smallest parts of the tasks. Although Mr. Green modified curriculum expectations, Evan was still visibly frustrated by the assignments provided. Mr. Green was unwilling to modify the curriculum any more than he had as he believed that if he did so Evan would never "catch up" to grade level expectations and needed to apply himself further. The one-on-one support Mr. Green tried to provide Evan with the work assigned was often greeted with hostility and rejection. Evan used the extra time provided to simply do nothing and instead incessantly fidget with his hands inside his desk. Mr. Green frequently reminded him to get back on task and remove his hands from the inside of his desk. These reminders and redirections did nothing to improve Evan's performance, engagement, or their relationship. Mr. Green felt simultaneously helpless and amazed by the degree to which his colleagues, the student record, the assessments, and the experts had defined and predicted what he was experiencing with Evan. It seemed that they were right and that he would simply have to manage his expectations and patience for Evan. However, Mr. Green was to be surprised when he began a novel study with his class.

The novel study co-decided by the class was *Sadako and the Thousand Paper Cranes* by Eleanor Coerr. The main character, Sadako, has leukemia due to radiation exposure during Hiroshima. Throughout her time in the hospital she tries to make 1,000 origami paper cranes in accordance with a

Japanese legend and its belief that doing so would grant her wish to live. Mr. Green read occasional chapters aloud beginning with the first one and had students read other chapters independently. He recorded himself reading the novel chapter by chapter and provided this recording to Evan who would listen to it with earphones while following along with his copy of the novel. After the second chapter, Evan surprisingly approached Mr. Green. He tentatively and quietly asked, "Mr. Green, can we make paper cranes?"

Evan flipped to the very last page of the book and showed Mr. Green the illustrated step by step instructions provided. For the first time Evan seemed interested in something and the only time he initiated interaction with Mr. Green.

Shocked by his request, Mr. Green replied, "Sure, Evan. Let's finish the book and then make the cranes."

Evan seemed satisfied enough with Mr. Green's response and returned to his desk. Throughout the weeks that followed, Evan listened to the novel as recorded by Mr. Green but had to be reminded and sternly reprimanded for fidgeting in his desk while doing so. The fidgeting continued throughout the day as well.

"Hands on desk, Evan."

"Stop fidgeting, Evan."

"I need to see your hands, Evan."

"Where should your hands be, Evan?"

"Get your hands out of your desk, Evan."

Mr. Green's increasing frustration with Evan made him contemplate whether he should use the crane activity as a consequence. If Evan didn't stop fidgeting he would not allow him to participate in making the cranes, or better yet, the entire class wouldn't make the cranes period. This seemed a preferable course of action as Mr. Green himself had made several unsuccessful attempts at making the paper cranes in preparation for the activity. He thought that he needed to be able to demonstrate the art to the class before allowing them to do so. Yet each time he tried to make a crane, he failed. Although he examined the illustrated instructions carefully repeatedly and followed them precisely, all of these attempts ended badly and with paper creatures that looked nothing like cranes. Why bother? he thought. If this is too difficult for me, how will the kids do it and why should we? Evan's behavior didn't warrant a reward.

As the last chapter ended, more students became aware of the last page and also asked whether the class would make paper cranes. Despite his previous thoughts, Mr. Green declared, "Tomorrow. We will make them in art class tomorrow." He shot a quick look at Evan who was grinning slightly. This was the only time throughout the past two months he had witnessed Evan looking even remotely happy because of anything he had done or said.

That night Mr. Green again tried to make a paper crane. Despite his numerous attempts all he had achieved was becoming progressively more agitated to the point of swearing and ripping his origami failures to pieces. Before going to bed, he looked around his apartment and saw mounds of crumpled up, ripped and shredded paper everywhere. He had no idea what he was going to do tomorrow. Art class was going to go very badly. He just knew that his class would be as frustrated as he was while trying to make the cranes, if not more. Evan, who didn't deserve to make the cranes, would assuredly be the most frustrated of all and that would only advance his disengagement, poor performance and lack of focus. If only he hadn't promised Evan and the class that they would make these ridiculous cranes, he thought, as he tossed and turned while trying to fall asleep.

Exasperated and exhausted, Mr. Green began art class during the last period of the next day with much dread. Although he anticipated that a colossal disaster was about to happen, he did not know what to do and as such, simply told his students to make a crane using the paper he gave them and the instructions provided at the back of the novel. With that, he distributed the paper. He started with Evan's group figuring that this would give Evan a head start. He also hoped that a member of Evan's group would perhaps be able to make one and then help him.

Once Mr. Green finished handing out the paper to all his students, he sighed, closed his eyes for a second, and begrudgingly turned to head to the group where Evan sat. He suddenly stopped inches away from Evan's desk, which now had a perfectly made paper crane sitting on it. Evan was, however, out of his seat. Mr. Green tried to quickly process what was happening. He paused then pointed to the crane and with a surprised tone asked, "Evan, did you make that?"

"Ya," Evan said softly.

Mr. Green finished walking over to Evan's desk where he picked up the crane and marvelled at it before putting it down. He then looked directly at Evan and said, "It's perfect."

Evan stared at Mr. Green briefly and then darted his eyes back to one of his groupmates who chimed in, "He's helping me make mine."

Mr. Green watched closely as Evan carefully helped a groupmate make a crane. Evan was patient and kind. He said very little but complimented what had been done with very few words and then showed where there was a problem and what to do next. He took his own crane and unfolded it to the place where his groupmate had trouble. He then slowly refolded it from that point, showing each step and fold as his groupmate followed along. Evan's other classmates saw this and asked for his help. Evan left his group and circulated around the classroom helping every classmate who needed it, each time doing the same thing Mr. Green had observed.

"This is good. This folds here. See. Ya. Good."

Mr. Green took a seat and watched. He was still and silent. Students who had made a crane with Evan's help asked Mr. Green for more paper so they could make one completely by themselves. He handed out more paper, sat back down and watched quietly as his students busily and contentedly made paper cranes. All the while Evan continued to circulate around the room helping his classmates. Some of the students Evan had helped were now offering assistance to others in the exact same way Evan had. "You got this part. Nice. Evan showed me how you do this part. See. It folds here. Good."

Based on all of this, Mr. Green made a decision. He stood up from where he was sitting and announced clearly so that the class could hear. "Evan, I am wondering if you could help me make a crane. I can't do it. I tried many times last night and couldn't."

The class was silent. Evan finished helping his classmate, walked over to Mr. Green, and as he had with his peers, began to kindly, gently, and patiently guide Mr. Green through the process of making a crane all the while using his own crane to demonstrate. Mr. Green sat beside Evan and carefully watched, followed, and folded his paper just as Evan was teaching him to. Mr. Green finally made a crane with Evan's help while some of his students pretended not to stare.

"What should we do with the cranes, Mr. Green?" asked the class.

"Let's tape string to them and I'll hang them from the ceiling. Tomorrow when you walk in, your cranes will be above your desks," replied Mr. Green.

It was now the end of the day, which meant agendas, reminders, handing out forms for an upcoming trip, and finally dismissal. When his students were gone, Mr. Green closed his classroom door, sat at his desk, and stared at his paper crane for a while. He then stood up almost involuntarily, walked over to Evan's desk, and attempted to sit in his small chair. As his knees hit the top of the desk, Evan's perfect paper crane jumped up and fell on the floor. As Mr. Green leaned over to pick it up, he noticed that the desk was full of paper cranes. Some were decorated beautifully. He began pulling out the cranes one by one to look at them more closely. He discovered other things. Evan had made a tiny bed that had a cut out illustration of a girl lying on it. He found tiny pieces of paper with drawings on them. Some of these illustrations were birds and others were what he recognized to be events from *Sadako and the Thousand Paper Cranes*, as well as a number of other animals that he realized were in texts the class had read before the novel study began.

Mr. Green then opened Evan's journal and paged through it. Although he collected and read his students' journals frequently, this time the entry that read "I like cranes" was much more significant. He saw other illustrations that also made more sense to him now. The illustrations were related to things that they had done in class. Previously, he had mostly ignored these illustrations.

Mr. Green had taught primary grades and knew the importance of providing young children with a journal with space on the top of the page for illustrations, but when he was assigned grade four, he purchased notebooks that only contained lines as grade four students would surely not need a space to draw. Although he did not forbid Evan to draw, he focused his attention on the limited or non-existent print descriptions underneath the illustrations. He was now seeing these drawings and the effort and thought Evan had put into them and began to realize what he must actually have been doing with his hands in his desk. Mr. Green thought about the many times he had harshly scolded Evan for fidgeting.

Overcome with shame, Mr. Green pushed the tiny chair he was sitting on away from Evan's desk and fully covered his face with his hands. For the first time ever in his classroom, he began to sob and he could not stop despite fears that one of his colleagues, or worse, the principal would walk into his classroom at any moment.

Eventually Mr. Green calmed himself, took a deep breath, stood up, wiped his tears with his shirt sleeve, and put everything back into Evan's desk. He walked over to the sink where the coarse brown paper towels hung and looked at himself in the stainless steel dispenser as he washed his very red face. He sat at his own desk and began to write. He wanted to remember what had just happened but rather than describe it, he made a list of all of the things he had discovered about Evan that afternoon and how they could help him teach him. When he read what he wrote, he realized that nothing he had read in books about MID, nothing that Evan's previous teachers had said, nothing in Evan's school record, nothing in Evan's tests and assessments, and nothing that he previously thought about Evan until that moment resembled the information he had just written. He then hung all of the paper cranes his students had left on their desks, collected his things, shut the lights of the classroom, went home, and fell into bed.

That night he dreamt that the paper cranes had broken free from their strings and were flying around the classroom. Mr. Green saw himself backing away from the cranes looking fearful. His students, however, were joyous and delighted by them. No one was more enthralled by what was happening than Evan who stood completely still with his mouth open in awe watching them fly above his head. Suddenly, they all landed on Evan's shoulders and began to lift him up by his shirt. They flew him around the room and Evan's classmates cheered as they made their way toward an open window. Mr. Green realized what was happening, quickly ran toward them, and grabbed hold of Evan's legs. The cranes fluttered their wings quicker than they had been and tried determinedly to escape out the window with Evan. Mr. Green pulled harder until Evan was standing on the floor and the cranes relented.

He then quickly closed the window. As he did, the cranes returned to hanging from the ceiling on the strings they had broken free from.

Mr. Green had yard duty the next morning. He watched Evan and his classmates play in the field, something he had never done before. He noticed that Evan's classmates asked him to make the teams and that he even sorted out occasional conflicts and questionable plays quickly with just a few words. Although he was very small, he was also very fast and observant. At one point, Evan noticed Mr. Green watching and cheering him on and quickly looked away. What he previously had observed was that his students liked Evan well enough but never really displayed the kind of enthusiasm for him they reserved for other classmates who were smarter, taller, and more confident. These were the children who seemed to be good at everything and were not always patient with Evan when he needed help.

When the bell rang and everyone lined up to go inside, Mr. Green passed by Evan and let him know he thought he had done a great job playing and refereeing. Evan smiled briefly and then quickly darted his gaze away from Mr. Green.

As his class entered the room, they looked up at the paper cranes hanging above their desks. They pointed to each other's cranes and talked contentedly as they settled in to begin a new day. Mr. Green's crane was hanging above his desk as well.

"I just want to begin today by thanking Evan for all his help yesterday. I could not have made my crane without him. He also helped so many of you. He was such a great teacher. Thank you."

The class broke out in applause and cheers for Evan who blushed, smiled, and looked down at his desk.

A few days later Evan approached Mr. Green and initiated a conversation just as everyone was leaving the room for recess. This was the first time this had happened since asking to make the paper cranes. "Cranes make sounds to warn other cranes about enemies. I found out other stuff about cranes too."

"Would you like to share what you know with the class, Evan?" asked Mr. Green. Evan nodded silently.

"Over the past few days I've been learning a lot, too," said Mr. Green. He then proceeded to tell Evan about what he saw during the crane lesson, the beautifully decorated cranes and illustrations he found in his desk, what he saw at recess, and all of the things he was noticing about Evan that he hadn't before. "I want you to know that I understand now what you were doing with your hands in your desk." He then paused, took a deep breath, and said "I'm sorry." He then paused again and added, "You've been very busy!" With that Mr. Green let out a big laugh and told Evan he was glad he wanted to share what he knew about cranes.

Evan smiled and for the first time his eyes did not dart to the floor. He turned toward the door and left the classroom to join his classmates for recess.

Mr. Green's students began sharing things they knew about a variety of topics they were interested in, which led to individual and group projects that were presented to other classes as well. Evan's projects contained detailed illustrations that he displayed with great pride.

Mr. Green began to feel markedly different. His thoughts were different. How he described his students was different. What he did with them was different. His class/classroom was different and he was beginning to feel that he was finally becoming the kind of teacher he hoped he would be when he entered teaching. He also read and processed information about MID and Evan very differently. The image of his crane would appear to him whenever he was confronted by how hopeless MID and Evan was. The list Mr. Green made about Evan got longer as the year progressed. He made these lists about his other students as well.

Mr. Green met with the special education teacher and with humility, shared what had happened, what he learned and what he was doing because of it. He wondered if the help Evan was getting could be tied into the things he had discovered and changes he had made especially since Evan and the special education teacher seemed to have such a good relationship. At first the special education teacher was hesitant. She felt that Evan would benefit more from the intensive phonics instruction she had been providing. She did admit, however, that he was not making progress. She even shared that she had witnessed Evan trying so hard to sound out words that he moved his finger across and then past a line of text he was reading onto the end of the table as the sounds of the letters he was making were longer than the text on the page. She eventually offered to give what Mr. Green had outlined a try.

Throughout the remainder of the year, not everything was as perfect as Evan's paper crane. There were moments of frustration and Mr. Green did not always know what to do. It was, however, clear that Evan was happier, much more engaged, and present. This was also noticed by his mother at home, who Mr. Green began to communicate with much more frequently after the paper crane lesson. He asked questions about what Evan was like at home, what he enjoyed doing, and was good at. He also would occasionally phone her to share successes Evan was having at school. Evan's mother said it was the first time a teacher had called just to share good news.

Mr. Green would remember what had occurred during that art class many times throughout the year and the years that followed. Everything he read, heard, and the professional development he undertook was very much informed by what he experienced that day. The paper crane he made with Evan's help was kept in the top drawer of his desk as a reminder of what was important.

## DISCUSSION

If inclusion is to be philosophically understood, its epistemological nature needs to be made explicit. Epistemology is concerned with knowing, understanding, and theorizing how we know/come to know and what we consider "knowledge." As previously mentioned, an asset-oriented (Heydon & Iannacci, 2008) model of inclusion recognizes and capitalizes on people's assets and ways of knowing. This way of conceptualizing inclusion necessitates that disability be understood as a construct that requires repositioning from deficiency to valued knowledge. Disability must be seen as making valuable contributions to the epistemological diversity that exists within schools. As such, inclusion is much more than a model, practice, or strategy; it is an understanding of diverse ways of being and knowing. Rather than continuing to require and rely on studies that repeatedly affirm that students with disabilities do not negatively impact "other" students academically in inclusive classrooms (e.g., Dessemontet & Bless, 2013), educators need to think about and explore disability as an epistemology that allows learning communities to garner insights into ways of knowing and being that they would not otherwise have. This knowledge is essential and educative and its denial contributes to the marginalization and miseducation of students.

Inclusion is not only an ethical project because it is committed to respecting and responding to people with disabilities, but also because it fosters understandings of students that challenge and disrupt ableist sensibilities developed in environments where disability is rendered invisible as a way of knowing and undesirable as a way of being. Carlson (2010) notes how difficult developing this perspective can be given the challenges people with disabilities may have in *articulating* their standpoint and identity and the fact that our current understandings of epistemology are founded on a *certain kind* of knowledge. In order for this to be addressed so that epistemological diversity is valued within and vital to inclusive environments, we need to interrogate what is meant by *articulation* and the "*certain kind of knowledge*" we presently privilege. This interrogation is necessary if we are to disrupt the dominant discourses that have and continue to shape what students with disabilities experience in school settings. Students like Evan show us that privileged modes of communication within schools (spoken, written) marginalize and subjugate ways of knowing and ways of showing knowledge and as such, do not allow classroom spaces to embrace and forward semiotic diversity. Importantly, this is not a question of understanding the needs of "visual learners." Epistemological and semiotic variance is not a question of addressing "multiple intelligences" (Gardner, 1983). It is far more than that. It is about allowing for, validating, furthering and cultivating students' voices, their identities and their ways of knowing. This form of responsiveness to students is necessary if we are to attempt to understand their standpoint, their world view, their experiences and who they are. Just like Mr. Green, we must become critically reflective of the limited and limiting ways in which our privileging and investment in certain kinds of knowledge have prevented us from seeing who our students are. In short, we must become aware of and work to counter our inherent ableism and understand what factors and forces create and perpetuate it.

Cummins (2001) notes that important critically reflective processes enable teachers to recognize the ways in which deficit and medical model understandings and language frame and position students with disabilities. This framing informed Mr. Green's interactions within the *Evan's Paper Crane* narrative.

> [C]oercive relations of power can only operate through the micro-interactions between educators and students. Thus, educators, students, and communities can challenge this coercive process. Although educational and social structures will impose constraints on resistance, these structures can never stifle the pursuit of empowering interactions on the part of educators and students. In short, educators always have options in the way they negotiate identities with students and communities. (Cummins, 2001, p. 203, original emphasis)

Dominant discourses and the relations of power that inform notions of and responses to disability constantly permeate and circulate within schools. The positioning and identity of students like Evan deemed disabled are framed in ways that proliferate deficiency and defectiveness. The biomedical perspectives evident in the government and academic texts accessed by Mr. Green worked to ensure that this deficit framing and limited/limiting "identity options" (Cummins, 2005) were constantly reinforced. This framing becomes reiterated and present in teachers' assessments and language about students, thus further fossilizing their deficient identity and subsequently leading to them being assigned deficit-oriented and deficient pedagogies that further disable them (e.g., the synthetic, scope and sequenced, fragmented, context-reduced phonics instruction provided to Evan). The entire focus of this positioning and pedagogy is on everything that is perceived to be wrong with the child as language and content in official and unofficial information exchanged about him or her is deficit-oriented. There is little or no attention paid to the child's identity, what assets they possess and therefore what particular pedagogical approaches would benefit, capitalize on and further cultivate his/her assets. Throughout the course of trying to learn about who a child with a disability is, what is often provided, discovered and internalized instead is what the child is not, and what the child is deemed not to be is "normal" and capable. Further, this repetitive and problematic information does not provide information that actually enables teachers to understand who the child is and how to work with, respond to, and provide for them. As we saw with Evan, such deficit-focused positioning was internalized and manifested in his level of engagement and well-being. Deficit-oriented identities assigned to students like Evan manifests in their behavior, performance, and socio-emotional well-being. When relationships and pedagogies are informed and designed by deficit thinking, students and teachers demonstrate, perform, and internalize this deficiency. This has a direct impact on a student's ability to learn, grow, and develop relationships where epistemological growth, respect and diversity can be cultivated and fostered.

Although Cummins's assertion that educators can challenge coercive relations of power and the damaging and disabling effects they have on student and educator interactions is astute, what also needs to be noted is that the discourses informing macro interactions that impact micro interactions within classrooms need to be named, understood, contextually and critically reflected upon, destabilized, and rejected by educators. It was only after Mr. Green was confronted by how problematic everything he had internalized was that he was able to think, talk, and teach differently. Shifts in thought, language, and practice first and foremost require a direct confrontation with ableist, deficit, and biomedical model discourses that are replete within education. Dean (1992) argues that any "action against poverty must perhaps begin by deconstructing 'poverty' and 'the poor'" (p. 79). Similarly, any actions for or with students deemed disabled must begin with a thoughtful and critical deconstruction of what disability is and how we have deemed those identified as disabled. The talk and texts (both official and unofficial) framing disability and students with disabilities therefore requires reconceptualizing. This necessitates a shift from deficit, biomedical perspectives to critical, social, and asset-oriented understandings of disability/people with disabilities that recognize disability as an important contributor to the identities people with disabilities have and the epistemologies they possess.

Kang (2008) points out that "very little research has investigated the relationship between personal epistemologies and teaching" (in Brownlee, Schraw, and Berthelsen, 2011, p. 4). As such, a "gap seems to be evident in the area of personal epistemologies and teaching practice at all levels—early years, elementary, secondary, and tertiary teaching with research into teacher education even more limited" (Feucht, 2009, in Brownlee, Schraw, and Berthelsen, 2011, p. 4). There has been some research (Jordan & Stanovich, 2003) that explores the links between teachers' epistemologies and their responses to students with disability. This research has demonstrated that "epistemologies influence both beliefs about disability and practices in teaching for diversity [and] changing . . . practices requires a change in personal epistemologies and beliefs about disabilities. . ." (Brownlee, Schraw, and Berthelsen, 2011, p. 11). Adding to the problem is that some of the limited research that does exist has depicted teachers' epistemological beliefs about disability as a binary. Jordan et al. (2010), for example, interviewed teachers about their understandings of disability using a protocol that identified their beliefs as pathognomonic or interventionist. Pathognomonic beliefs position disability as an inherent pathological condition identified through medical identification. Teachers who expressed these beliefs were said to understand disability as something that could not be helped and therefore they were not responsible for fostering student learning. Further, they were said to have preferred that students with disabilities were withdrawn from the classroom for instruction geared toward their disability. Teachers with interventionist beliefs see disability as resulting from barriers and ableist environments and believe they are responsible for removing these barriers. They also prefer that resources be delivered in the classroom to assist them with students with disabilities. The pathognomonic/interventionist binary inherent in the Jordan et al. (2010) study also characterized teachers deemed to have interventionist beliefs as working at higher levels of instructional interaction and engagement with all their students as well as with those with disabilities than those with pathognomonic beliefs.

Although the Jordan et al. (2010) study is helpful in demonstrating the relationship between beliefs about disability and instruction, the *Evan's Paper Crane* narrative demonstrates further complexity than depicted by the pathognomonic/interventionist distinction. For example, although Mr. Green demonstrated pathognomonic internalized beliefs that were a result of the dominant biomedical discourse present in the official and unofficial texts and talk he sought out about Evan and his MID, he believed that it was his responsibility to teach him. In fact, the reason why biomedical discourses and deficit-oriented perspectives were able to inform his thinking and approach to Evan was because he desperately sought out various information sources as a result of wanting to learn how to teach him. Further, although Mr. Green's initial pathognomonic beliefs were disrupted, this did not necessitate abandoning withdrawal support for Evan, but rather working collaboratively with the special education teacher to create more meaningful and engaging instruction based on Evan's assets and interests.

What the Jordan et al. (2010) study also does not address is the standardized context in which schools presently operate. As previously mentioned, Dudley-Marling (2004) points out that "no student can have LD [learning disabilities] on his or her own. It takes a complex system of interactions performed in just the right way, at the right time, on the stage we call school" (p. 489). The neoliberal education policy context that insists on standardized curriculum and assessment, positions teachers and students in ways that further complicate beliefs about and responses to disability. Allowing students a safe space to receive engaging instruction away from the tyranny of standards provides them with personalized, one-on-one instruction that is focused on their needs. With a collaborative approach, the skills, strategies, and content offered to the students need not be focused on pathologies. The important aspect absent from the current discussion and conceptualizations about/of inclusion is the nature of the support being offered to students with disabilities. Yet, this is the conversation that is required if schools and teachers are to create truly inclusive learning environments that are responsive to student needs rather than superficial understandings about what inclusion is or is not. Although Schwartz & Jordan's more recent study (2011) also demonstrates important links between teachers' epistemological beliefs about disability and their teaching practices, the binary analysis and depiction of inclusion continues to ignore the contextually informed and idiosyncratic ways in which teachers come to these beliefs and how these beliefs can be disrupted. Reconceptualization demands that educators carefully consider what is pedagogically offered to students with disabilities and how these offerings can be based on their assets and challenges.

We are becoming aware of the complexity involved in destabilizing dominant discourses, thinking, language and practices with respect to disability and students with disabilities. Paugh & Dudley-Marling (2011), for example, revealed how difficult it was for novice teachers to "challenge the powerful discourse of schooling that situates school failure - and success - in students and their families" and to resist "the deficit language that dominates the discourse of school failure" (p. 13) despite the fact that these novice teachers participated in several bi-weekly inquiry group meetings over the course of a year designed to help them shift from a deficit to an asset-oriented gaze regarding students who struggle. Paugh & Dudley-Marling (2011) concluded that it was necessary for teacher education to "raise awareness about discourse, [and] help teachers to use such knowledge to assume positions of authority and provide tools for challenging, rather than defaulting to, deficit discourses surrounding learning diversity." (p. 14). Graham & Iannacci (2013) also found that teacher candidates had not fully internalized asset-oriented theoretical perspectives and language that had been modeled for and incorporated by them during a "Special Education" course they were required to take during their Bachelor of Education that had and an accompanying tutoring practicum with learners who had special needs. Data was collected in survey form before the course began and when the course was over. Further focus group sessions were conducted that allowed teacher candidates to discuss what they had learned about literacy, disabilities, and the learners they tutored.

Focus group discussions revealed that course understandings were abandoned when teacher candidates were immersed in school cultures that entrenched institutionalized ways of defining and knowing students with disabilities. These teacher candidates saw firsthand and understood that schools were required to measure students' abilities and progress using standardized curriculum expectations and tests. They also observed how schools were mandated to use deficit medical model informed policies, procedures, and definitions of disabilities in order for students to be tested by the school board or outside agency personnel and formally identified as having a disability in order to determine an accompanying placement and subsequently have access to resources and funding. Teacher candidates became complicit with this world view as they participated in dominant discourses that reinforce ableism. This assimilation is exacerbated by the fact that teacher candidates are seeking employment and therefore feel pressure to acquire the values, beliefs, language, and practices present within schools.

The Graham & Iannacci (2013) study also explored through a critically reflexive process that the researchers were also responsible for inadvertently promoting and propagating a deficit-based model since a major assignment teacher candidates were to complete required them to concentrate on a disability rather than keeping the focus on a child who had a disability. The disability rather than the child was the focal point of the assignment and, as such, one of the reasons dominant notions about disability remained unchallenged by teacher candidates. In addition, teacher candidates were referred to and expected to use official government required texts to complete the assignment. Despite efforts to promote a critical reading of these texts, teacher candidates assimilated official definitions and dominant discourses of disability present within these texts. Being critically reflexive of their own practice allowed Graham & Iannacci (2013) to reconceptualize the assignment in order to combat the notion that exceptionalities were simply lists of deficits that needed to be located in students and responded to generically. Teacher candidates were now required to create student-centered asset-oriented case studies that focused on a student with an exceptionality by first identifying the student's assets and a few challenges based on some of the characteristics of the specific exceptionality. The process then enables instructional responses that are respectful of and responsive to students' assets and needs, rather than an essentialist understanding of their disability.

The next chapter focuses on the nature of these instructional responses. Importantly, it examines intersections between literacy and disability and uses multiliteracies perspectives to reconfigure these intersections within education in ways that are respectful of and responsive to the literacies people with disabilities possess. Pedagogical approaches informed by multiliteracies perspectives are provided as alternatives to the limited and limiting understandings of literacy/literacy pedagogy currently assigned people who have disabilities within education.

## NOTE

1. These or similar phrases and expectations appear in a variety of standardized curriculum documents and frameworks throughout Canada, the US, and the UK.

# Chapter Four

# Literacy, Disability, Pedagogy, and Practice

What would happen, they conjectured, if they simply went on assuming their children would do *everything*. Perhaps not quickly. Perhaps not by the book. But what if they simply erased those growth and development charts, with their precise, constricting points and curves? What if they kept their expectations but erased the time line? What harm could it do? Why not try?

—Kim Edwards, *The Memory Keeper's Daughter*, 2005

Previous chapters demonstrate ways in which dominant discourses in education problematically configure disability and inclusion. The narratives thus far have illuminated the lived experiences of students, teachers, administrators and education professors in relation to limited and limiting understandings of disability and inclusion.[1] The ways in which students with disabilities are positioned and provided illustrates how dominant disability discourses impact thinking about language and pedagogy. The Spedcycle (see Figure 4.1), attempts to capture the ways in which pathologizing processes lead to problematic responses and how official and unofficial texts, tools, and talk continue to ensure that this cycle remains unbroken.

**Figure 4.1. Current Special Education Cycle = The Spedcycle**

1) Students with disabilities are deficient and incapable.

2) We must measure their deficiencies and identify their pathologies.

3) Results verify that students with disabilities are deficient and in need of fixing.

4) We can fix students with disabilities using certain interventions.

5) Subject students with disabilities to these disabling interventions.

6) Measure them again after receiving these interventions.

7) Results provide further evidence that #1 is correct. The cycle continues.

*Discourse and Dollars

*What fuels the cycle[2]

## THE SPEDCYCLE EXPLAINED

1. The dominant disability discourse that informs official and unofficial texts as well as talk in education references biomedical models of disability. Disability is represented as an inherent flaw in individuals rather than as a disabling social construct and constellation of practices.
2. The tools used to measure disability are devoid of meaningful, meaning-making opportunities. Their creation and continued use is based on the idea that intelligence, achievement, and development can be numerically and objectively represented using these tools.

3. Disability therefore becomes something that is hunted using tools designed to create and find it. These tools and the thinking underpinning them are forwarded and left unchallenged.
4. Once a pathology is identified, a cure may be found. Interventions abound and are made available to those identified as having the identified pathology.
5. Such interventions focus on isolating deficiencies and are designed to address them in a context-reduced manner. As such they further pedagogically poor experiences for people subjected to them.
6. Measuring student progress post intervention using similarly problematic tools further ensures that people with disabilities are understood to be deficient.
7. Discourses, texts, tools, and talk remain deficit-focused and enable the spedcycle to continue.

Previous chapters have mapped the thinking, language, placements, and practices that may counter the spedcycle. The remainder of this chapter explores how limited and limiting ways of understanding literacy and therefore identifying those who are considered literate, have influenced the forms of literacy pedagogy assigned, and resigned to people with disabilities. Multiliteracies theory is used to help reconceptualize "asset-oriented" (Heydon & Iannacci, 2008) understandings of inclusion, literacy, and pedagogy as they relate to people with disabilities. These alternative pedagogical models and principles are specifically explored as are necessary professional supports, structures, and ethics that forward inclusive environments that enable such pedagogy.

## LITERACY AND PERSONHOOD

Kliewer, Biklen, and Kasa-Hendrickson (2006) have clearly shown how people with disabilities have been denied personhood as a result of being thought of as illiterate and thus incapable of demonstrating literacy. These authors interrogate the problematic idea that "citizenship in the literate community is an organic impossibility for people defined as intellectually disabled" (p. 163). Through a critical exploration of various historic cases and figures, they demonstrate "literate invisibility as a product of cultural dehumanization" (p. 167). Dominant disability discourses and print and verbo-centric understandings of literacy have contributed to this invisibility and "cultural denial of competence" (p. 163). Historically, literacy has and continues to be understood as the ability to use print, the technology of the spoken word, and as such, something that can be articulated or represented in orthographically sanctioned ways (e.g., an alphabetic system). The New London Group (1996) has disrupted these ideas and helped render visible the various kinds of literacies people possess. The shift from thinking about literacy as singular to understanding it as multiple encapsulates this dynamic redefining of literacy.

Two major aspects of multiliteracies are (1) the variability of meaning-making in different cultural, social, or professional contexts and (2) how meaning is made in ways that are increasingly multimodal and involve interactions with a range of semiotic systems (written, visual, verbal, audio, spatial, non-verbal, e.g., silence, kinesics, proxemics) (Hornberger, 2000) and mediating devices (e.g., technology) (Gee, 2001). Meaning-making is dependent upon engagement with or creation of texts in order to make sense of and/or produce texts by using any number of modalities (Cope & Kalantzis, 2000).

An asset-oriented model of inclusion supports the notion that literacy is not just about the knowledge, acquisition, and use of a code, but a culture (Iannacci, 2007). The ways language and literacy develop, are understood and valued are shaped by their use within social contexts. Thus, how people understand, come to, and use literacy in particular social contexts and what they gain in so doing becomes a central concern for understanding what literacy is and what it does (Toohey, 2000). This perspective recognizes that texts are privileged and marginalized differently in different contexts. As culture creates what is understood and taken for granted about literacy, ableist sensibilities embedded in these understandings remain unchallenged. Therefore what has been sanctioned as literate behavior must be questioned when applied to and used against people with disabilities. Definitions of literacy must be opened up in order to reveal how people make meaning of the world with a variety of communicative options that do not necessarily require conventional print or verbal utterance. Understanding literacy in this way allows us to examine the values, mores, norms, and worldviews embedded in our current thinking, and also troubles what we know about and how we provide for students deemed disabled. This shift allows us to be conscious of how our use of specific terms and concepts compromise students' personhood and reifies their identities in ways that subject them to limited definitions and measured deficiencies. These perspectives also reveal the limited and limiting ways in which pedagogies assigned to students with disabilities based on narrow notions of literacy have supported the special education/regular education binary (Heydon & Iannacci, 2008) and processes of pathologization that result in pedagogical determinism (Iannacci, 2018) [wherein students with disabilities are assigned and resigned to fragmented, rote-oriented, context-reduced literacy curricula] (Barone, 2002, Delpit, 2003, Iannacci, 2008). Therefore we must no longer focus on whether placement options are in-line with inclusion, but rather think critically about the quality of instruction offered to students in a variety of placement options from which they may benefit.

Any placement option deemed best for students with disabilities must be questioned in terms of what it is offering them. This questioning is vital given the pedagogically impoverished instruction (Iannacci, 2018) that has often been provided to students with disabilities. Multiliteracies perspectives forward pedagogies that are dynamic and responsive to the various ways that students with disabilities make meaning and demonstrate their knowledge and identity. These perspectives are aligned with pedagogical foundations of inclusion such as universal design (UD) and differentiated instruction (DI). Universal design (UD) refers to instructional, environmental, and assessment strategies teachers can employ that may benefit all students (e.g., options for students to demonstrate knowledge verbally, visually, tactically, with print, etc.). Allowing students to use a variety of communication options to demonstrate what they know is universally beneficial to all students and reflects UD principles. Hehir (202) has noted that universal design features in architecture such as ramps and closed captioning have benefitted nondisabled people. Applying universal design to education has similarly been helpful to many students regardless of their dis/ability. Hehir (2002) has also noted that "as is the case with architecture, the failure to design universally is inefficient and ineffective" (p. 28) . . . and that "Universal design is a matter of simple justice" (p. 29). Differentiated instruction "is a term describing how teachers get to know their students and use students' strengths to help them learn or accomplish academic goals without needing a diagnosed reason to help (Robb in Gentry, 2016). Therefore, when students' particular ways of knowing require specific access to modalities that allow their knowledge to be demonstrated, instruction, assessment and the classroom environment can be specifically differentiated in order to respond to these demonstrations of knowledge and needs. Thus, instructional, assessment and environmental accommodations and modifications can be developed to ensure responsiveness to a specific learner rather than superficial compliance to a limited understanding of inclusion. Similarly, differentiated instruction is designed to respond to where the student is rather that where they are supposed to be in relation to standardized curriculum based on their age/grade. As such, academic goals in the form of expectations, outcomes, targets, core objectives, etc., are indicative of the students' zone of proximal development (Vygotsky, 1978) and as such achievable with instructional support so that eventually with time and practice, the student performs differentiated academic goals independently. A multiliteracies framework supports and allows for UD and DI to be pedagogically fostered within classrooms. This way of thinking about, fostering, and instructionally planning for literacy engagement should be the focus of our thinking about inclusion and the designing of inclusive learning environments. This is the type of instruction Mr. Green eventually understood and was able to design for Evan and his students as illustrated in the *Evan's Paper Crane* narrative in the previous chapter.

## CUEING SYSTEMS AND THE DISABLING OF STUDENTS

In order to forward inclusive learning environments informed by multiliteracies perspectives that are respectful and responsive to students with disabilities, there must be an understanding of literacy processes and systems and the ways in which they relate to pedagogical responses to students with disabilities. The passage offered in Box 4.1 (Bransford & Johnson, 1972), combined with subsequent discussion of the processes and systems used in an attempt to make sense of the passage demonstrates the experiences learners with disabilities can have within education. In addition it suggests what these experiences can tell us about ways to improve literacy instruction offered to them. It is important to point out that although the passage used in this demonstration is a print text, the systems and processes students use to read non-print texts are similar. As such, all of the cueing systems[3] required to make sense of a variety of texts regardless of modality (visual, gestural, auditory, etc.) will also be discussed in order to demonstrate their significance to literacies that need to be accessed and fostered in order to make meaning of texts. This is also an important point to demonstrate since cueing systems and reading processes have been understood primarily through a print-centric lens. These systems and processes therefore need to be viewed as essential resources for students with disabilities to access and develop as they engage with a variety of multimodal texts.

---

**Box 4.1**

---

A newspaper is better than a magazine. A seashore is a better place than the street. At first it is better to run than to walk. You may have to try several times. It takes some skill but it's easy to learn. Even young children can enjoy it. Once successful, complications are minimal. Birds seldom get too close. Rain, however, soaks in very fast. Too many people doing the same thing can also cause problems. One needs lots of room. If there are no complications, it can be very peaceful. A rock will serve as an anchor. If things break loose from it, however, you will not get a second chance.

Failing to understand the meaning of this passage does not mean that you have a disability. However, the lack of a provided context (in this case, the title) is reminiscent of the type of instruction frequently assigned to students who have disabilities that render them disabled. It is therefore the instruction (or lack thereof) that is actually disabling. In this passage, not providing a title disables the reader from using all of the cueing systems necessary to make sense of the passage and therefore the processes required to actually read it. What is meant by reading the passage needs clarifying. If you made your way through the passage without difficulty but came to the end and still did not know what it meant, you decoded rather than read the passage. Reading requires sense making (Rich, 1998). Without being able to make sense of the passage, you were not able to read it. Decoding is not reading, yet literacy instruction provided for students with disabilities is frequently so decoding-focused that it actually disables their ability to read, and as such, make sense of texts. The instruction provided privileges and focuses so much attention on certain cueing systems believed to be pivotal for "them" to focus on, that all of the meaning-making assets they possess and are required to use to read texts are not accessed. It is necessary to explore the systems used while attempting to read the passage in order to understand what disabling instruction does to students already identified as disabled.

## THE ORTHOGRAPHIC SYSTEM

As you decoded the passage, you relied on your knowledge of the shape or the architecture of the letters you encountered. This is indicative of the orthographic system. The orthographic system is focused on the visual structure and formation of letters. A learner's ability to use this resource is based on their knowledge of letters and letter patterns, understanding of systems of spelling, and fine-motor skills. This is the system that allowed you to know what the letters in each of the words in the passage were. Similarly, if this were a graphic symbol, you would have relied on your knowledge of its shape to provide you with a sense of what it is or does.

## THE GRAPHOPHONIC SYSTEM

You also knew what sound the letters made as the graphophonic system enabled you to apply this knowledge. The graphophonic system is focused on a learner's knowledge of symbol-sound relationships (graphophonics) and therefore their ability to hear, sequence, segment, and blend together the smallest units in a spoken word (phonemes). Similarly, readers have knowledge about texts associated with certain sounds, which aids their ability to make meaning of these texts but by itself does not ensure meaning-making. You experienced this as you attempted to read the passage because even though you were able to use orthographic and graphophonic knowledge to decipher letters, the sounds they make and therefore what words were in the passage, you still were not able to read it.

## THE SYNTACTIC SYSTEM

You also undoubtedly stopped at periods, paused at commas, and read the passage with flow as you could predict what words would logically follow others. Here you used the syntactic system. This system is focused on the patterns of word order and/or grammar that helps determine meaning in sentences. A learner's ability to use this resource is based on their knowledge of the structure of language, awareness of sentence function and sense, and understanding of how words are ordered. Similarly, visual texts also have a structure and grammar of which readers have knowledge. This knowledge alone is insufficient in allowing them to read a visual text. In short, even though orthographic, graphophonic, and syntactic knowledge was activated and utilized as you tried to read the passage, you were unable to. All you could accomplish with the help of these systems was decoding the passage. Despite being detrimental to meaning-making, instruction provided for students with disabilities is often excessively focused on the orthographic and graphophonic system in particular.

## IMPLICATIONS FOR INSTRUCTION AND ASSESSMENT

An instructional focus on the orthographic and graphophonic systems is reinforced by the problematic idea that if letter formation is practiced incessantly accompanied by copious amounts of decontextualized phonics instruction, then students will build the skills to be able to read print. This is reminiscent of mastery learning (that one skill/strategy/concept must be mastered before attempting to learn the next one) and its false belief that skills and knowledge are incrementally attained and therefore need to be taught in succession. As such, a scope and sequence of what is to be focused on first is therefore possible to identify and instructionally isolate. Examples of this can be seen in phonics-focused programs such as *Jolly Phonics*, which provide a chronological order indicating what specific letters, letter combinations and vowels should be taught prior to others[4]. Interestingly the program has been praised for its use of pictures and gestures to reinforce symbol/sound knowledge. The gestures and pictures, however, are just as decontextualized as the letters it isolates and therefore just as meaningless. Further, some of the illustrations and gestures associated with letter/letter sounds are culturally and socioeconomically specific thus ensuring that the program is problematic for students in terms of its cognitive, cultural, language, and learning load (Meyer, 2000). Similarly, dominant and problematic notions about how to teach grammar (part of the syntactic system) isolates the teaching of nouns and verbs before subjects, predicates, and other parts of sentences/speech.

The problematic instructional focus on and privileging of the orthographic and graphophonic systems has meant that students with disabilities (and many other students)[5] have been subjected to numerous worksheets requiring them to trace or practice letters and fill in blanks with correct letters or identify correct letters at the beginning, end, or in the middle of words, and as such, are tasks that are cognitively undemanding yet difficult as they are devoid of context. Similarly, syntactic system-focused instruction isolates punctuation and grammar in ways that render it meaningless and non-transferable. Tasks that attempt to foster this system require students to add in missing punctuation or circle/underline various types of words (nouns, verbs, adjectives, etc.). Once again, these are cognitively undemanding tasks but because they are context-reduced (Cummins, 2005), they disable learners as they do not allow them to engage in meaning-making.

Schooling is unfortunately all too often dominated with tasks, black line masters, and programs that focus on the orthographic, graphophonic, and syntactic systems to the exclusion of other systems that are necessary for a reader to simultaneously use in order to successfully read a text. Although this form of instruction is also provided to students who don't have disabilities, it is especially prevalent in "interventions" deemed necessary for students with disabilities as it is believed that "they" need this form of instruction far more than their "normal" peers. In fact, actual reading in classrooms that involves opportunities to engage in meaning-making using or creating authentic texts and tasks is something that at times, only "normal" children are permitted to do. Assessment tools used to make these instructional decisions are often also designed to focus on specific cueing systems. When students with disabilities do not perform well on such assessments, they are understood to be in need of even more instruction that isolates and works on these particular systems. Here are, for example (Box. 4.2), some items from the Rosner Test of Auditory Analysis.

---

**Box 4.2**

---

Say "coat." Now say it again, but don't say /k/
Say "stale." Now say it again, but don't say /t/
Say "smack." Now say it again, but don't say /m/

---

The Rosner is the oldest published test of phonemic awareness (Torgesen & Mathes, 1999). Although this test was designed to test auditory analysis, it has been used to ascertain students' reading as phoneme segmentation is falsely believed to be a predictor of reading capabilities. Torgesen & Mathes (1999), for example, state that the "ultimate purpose for assessment of phonological awareness is to identify children who are likely to experience reading difficulties" (p. 9). Another very common reading assessment used in schools that is entirely focused on the graphophonic system (Table 4.1) requires students to identify a specific letter, tell the teacher what sound the letter makes and then say a word that begins with the letter.

**Table 4.1 Letter/Sound Recognition Assessment**

| Upper | Letter | Sound | Word | Lower | Letter | Sound | Word |
|-------|--------|-------|------|-------|--------|-------|------|
| A | √ | X | X | a | X | X | X |
| Etc. | | | | | | | |
| Total Correct:_____ | | | | Total Correct:_____ | | | |
| Comments:_____ | | | | | | | |

These assessments also highlight an interesting contradiction. Developmentalism has been problematic for students with disabilities as a result of its focus on identifying what is considered "normal" physical, emotional and cognitive growth. Although developmentalism is rooted in Piagetian theory, the focus of these assessments contradicts Piaget's own stages of cognitive development which follow a concrete to abstract trajectory. These assessments either focus exclusively on abstracts or begin with them. As such, they are devoid of concretes and context and therefore not only meaningless but a form of purposeless mental gymnastics that provides no useful information about a student's meaning-making abilities (their actual reading). A teacher I interviewed described these assessments and the tasks students were asked to complete while doing them as "tricky things" (Iannacci, 2005). Interestingly, the "tricky," limited and limiting nature of these assessments (and others like them) are not understood to be disabling.

What has not been fully realized is how context-reduced assessment and instruction ensures that students are unable to *actually* read. In other words, students' assessed or perceived inability to read is directly related to the fact that they have not been provided with anything that would enable them to do so. This disabling process is exactly what you experienced in decoding and not being able to read the untitled passage. Once you are, however, provided with the necessary contextual information to make sense of the passage, other cueing systems are accessed that will enable you to read it. In order to demonstrate this, consider and read the title of and contextual information about the passage that has been provided in Figure 4.2 and Figure 4.3. Once you have done so, go back and re-read the passage (Box 4.1).

**Figure 4.2. Making and Flying a Kite**

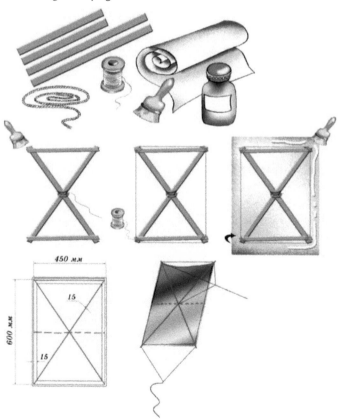

**Figure 4.3.  Flying a Kite**

Now that you have been given vital contextual information, you could
finally read the passage. Once the title, a set of labeled visual instructions and
a photo were provided, you knew that the passage would focus on making and
flying a kite. You were therefore better prepared to read the passage as you
understood its focus, purpose and particulars. This knowledge is what makes
up and helps activate the pragmatic cueing system.


## THE PRAGMATIC SYSTEM

This system is focused on the contextual/cultural specifics of language
use. A learner's ability to use this resource is based on their knowledge
of the social rules and conventions of language in a particular context. It
also requires and furthers their understanding of aspects of various genres
and forms (e.g., fairy tales, poems, weather reports, maps, etc.), as well as
their understanding of the syntax particular to various forms (e.g., newspaper headlines, recipes, warning signs, etc.). The pragmatic system helps
contextualize graphophonic knowledge and therefore renders it specific to
particular types of texts (e.g., the graphophonics of comics is different than
advertisements and environmental print). This system draws on and uses a
reader's awareness of the expectations of a text created by different authors
(e.g., reporter, scientist, advertiser, etc.). Therefore a sense and expectation
of the situation (e.g., reading for pleasure, informal or formal styles, etc.)
becomes important knowledge for readers to access as they try to make sense
of what they are reading. The title *Making and Flying a Kite* for example,

immediately tells a reader that this will be a how-to type of text and therefore will be structured in ways that explain the steps required in being able to do something. As such, the reader knows this is non-fiction and will be informational and, in the case of the above passage, procedural. Similarly, contextual information allows readers to understand what volume and vernacular is or isn't acceptable in specific spaces and places in relation to verbal texts.

## THE SEMANTIC SYSTEM

When contextual information is provided to allow the reader to utilize the pragmatic system, they are able to use other resources to make personal sense of and therefore fully connect with a text. This is indicative of the semantic system. The semantic system is focused on comprehension and meaning. A learner's ability to use this resource is based on their background knowledge, personal experiences, prior experience, and knowledge of the topic and familiarity with concepts. Once learners have contextualized a text and have linked the text to what they already know and have experienced, they are more apt to engage with the text in a critical way. This vital engagement with a text draws on and forwards the critical system.

## THE CRITICAL SYSTEM

The critical system is focused on implicit and applied understandings of text. A learner's ability to use this resource is based on their ability to explore what is taken for granted within a text and understand that all texts are not neutral. This necessitates questioning the biases, attitudes, values, and beliefs that lie beneath the surface in a text. Critical reading is of course not restricted to print texts, but is rather a necessary process to engage when reading any and all texts in whatever modality. When instruction does not enable assets, systems and processes that students have at their disposal and that are necessary to ensure reading, it remains decoding-focused. As a result of such disabling instruction, students are not provided with opportunities and therefore do not develop the necessary skills to be able to critically read. When you fully consider how vital critical reading is in the twenty-first century, you realize that students with disabilities who are often the recipients of disabling instruction are not only disadvantaged, but also placed "at risk." Comber (2011) points out the ways in which critical literacy has not been developed in students deemed deficient (specifically young children). Yet being able to critically read texts is necessary for survival. Without it, students with disabilities (all students) are left without the necessary ability to critically discern the various texts they encounter throughout their lives. This leaves them vulnerable to these texts and therefore further marginalized by a world they have been rendered unable to understand and navigate.

What has just been explored demonstrates the ways in which literacy instruction provided to students with disabilities directly affects the ways in which they are understood, assessed, provided for and positioned. The demonstration allowed you the reader to be placed in a situation that resembles that which students with disabilities encounter and experience as a result of problematic and disabling instruction that is antithetical to accessing and fostering the assets and literacies they bring with them into classrooms. What follows are pedagogical models, strategies and practices that reconceptualize instruction provided to students with disabilities in order to further explore alternatives. The whole-part-whole model will be described as it provides a way of organizing instruction that is context-focused. This model and pedagogy that stems from it draws on students' cueing systems, assets, and processes that enable them to access and develop their literacies.

## INSTRUCTIONAL ALTERNATIVES: THE
## WHOLE-PART-WHOLE MODEL

Pedagogy informed by the whole-part-whole model (Figure 4.4) is focused on meaning-making. As such, instruction begins with first exposing students to and immersing them in a variety of relevant multimodal whole texts (visual, behavioral, print-based etc.). This means selecting texts in which students are interested, demonstrate competence with, have challenges reading or creating and/or are necessary for the student to be able to understand and produce. Such texts access students' "funds of knowledge" (Moll, 1992) and thus their experiential and multimodal assets and challenges. Initial engagement with a text is context-embedded (Cummins, 2001) and focuses on learning with, through, and about the *whole* text. Once this immersion into a type of text has occurred and several examples have been provided to fully acquaint learners with it, instruction is focused on learning about how the *parts* of the text function in ways that contribute to meaning-making. This entails explicit teaching of a textual feature(s) or skills/strategies that learners need to understand and use to make sense of and create this type of text. The learning at this point is focused on how the parts of the texts function. Once learners understand the parts that make up the text, they are provided with opportunities to transfer what they have learned. They will therefore use or apply what they have been taught to read or create *whole* texts they have been immersed in and familiar with. Instruction at this point in the learning process is focused on enabling learners to apply what they learned with, through, and about texts.

Figure 4.4. Whole-Part-Whole Model

## Whole

### Learning with, through, and about whole texts.

### Part
### Learning about how the parts (textual features) function.

### Whole
### Learning to apply what was learned with, through, and about texts

- Whole: text immersion
- Part: text deconstruction and explicit skill/strategy instruction
- Whole: transfer/application/use of text knowledge

## EXAMPLES OF WHOLE-PART-WHOLE INSTRUCTION

When I have taught students with disabilities who have difficulty reading facial or gestural expressions, I have found it helpful to show them a series of images depicting a variety of facial expressions and gestures. We then discuss what the specific parts of an image (e.g., arm movement, positioning of eyebrows, shape of mouth) might be communicating. We might ask: What are some gestural clues that suggest the person is angry and so on? Once students have explored each of these parts and have a sense of what they are communicating, they create their own facial/gestural expressions and share them with their peers who then decipher their meaning. A discussion also ensues throughout the process about contradictions between what people are saying and their facial/gestural expressions, thus providing a critical understanding of duplicity and how/why it used.

Since students I once taught in a self-contained special education classroom were interested in UFO sightings, I chose a variety of selections about reported UFO sightings from around the world (Tunguska, for example) and immersed them in such texts. I read the text aloud, we read them together, and I provided audio versions of the selections for those students who needed them. We then discussed how they were written, identified their common structure, what type of texts they were, how we knew they were that type of text, and finally, discussed the bias of the author and what told us they believed the UFO sighting had occurred. Various graphic organizers were used to break down this textual information. My students even began to count the number of paragraphs the author offered as proof the sighting had occurred and compared that to the number of paragraphs that provided evidence of the opposite. They began to see patterns in the structure of the texts and how authors used structure and certain words and phrases to prove or disprove whether the sighting had happened. Once the class had a good sense of the various parts of this type of text, students were then given or found their own selections about UFO sightings and individually, in pairs, and in small groups began the same process of critically reading the texts as had been previously demonstrated and modeled.

Another time, I showed my students a series of commercials designed to appeal to their age group. At first I just asked that they watch them. They were then asked to note the things they noticed most and finally, to focus on all the things that had to be done to make the commercial. We made lists of all these parts of the commercial (e.g., lighting, edits, camera angles, music, etc.). Further, we discussed whether the commercial was good or not based on whether it had enticed them to buy the product since this was the purpose of this type of text. Students began to realize the intent of commercials and the work that goes into making this type of text. They became aware of how everything in the text was purposefully designed and decided upon to get people to buy the product. Once we had a good sense of the parts of the commercials and what they did, students then used this knowledge to design their own commercials for products that existed or that they created.

Students in a self-contained special education class I taught were of an age where they started to take and were interested in extending their use of public transportation (e.g., to go to shopping malls). As such, they wanted to know how to read bus schedules. I brought in several schedules from local service providers and we began to look at them. As the students perused and traded them, I asked them to note anything they made sense of, things they didn't understand, and things that the various schedules had in common. Once they identified various features in the schedules, we made lists of the things they saw, understood, or found confusing. Each of these were named, explained, and then used to help read the schedule. Parts of the bus schedules like the route destinations, the route branch indicator, departure and arrival time indicators, day of service information, etc., were all focused on to make sense of the schedule. We then developed questions that could be answered by using the schedule. Students then traded schedules and questions about them and worked in pairs to answer the questions by reading the schedule. Anchor charts that labeled and explained the parts of the schedule were left around the room so that students could refer to this information in case they needed reminders of what certain features in the bus schedules did.

It's important to reiterate that *all* cueing systems are important to access and develop (Bainbridge & Heydon, 2017). The Make and Fly a Kite demonstration by no means suggests that orthographic or graphophonic systems should not be taught. The key is the way in which they are taught. Bell & Jarvis (2002) have similarly pointed out that teaching methods that superficially isolate letters/sounds are ineffective. In contrast, teaching letter formation or symbol sound relationships using a whole-part-whole model once again (just as it has been applied in previous examples) means that what informs and initiates instruction is context. Therefore, if a particular text that lends itself to focusing on a particular letter/sound is read, viewed, or heard, then that is what will eventually be focused on once the text(s) have been explored and made sense of holistically. Then, students can engage in a number of multimodal experiences to help reinforce letter formation and symbol/sound recognition. One such activity is providing students with boxes that contain concrete items that begin with both the letter(s)/sound(s) being purposefully focused on and others that do not. Students can be asked to sort these items into those that begin with specific letter(s)/sound(s) from those that do not. Students might then make/create the letter(s) these items start with tactilely (e.g., through foam, sandpaper, wire, chalkboard, electronically, etc.) in order to label the items. Crucially, once students have a sense of the letter and its sound, they use this knowledge to read or create related texts which allows them to transfer what they have learned.

I have also organized whole-part-whole structured lessons that focus on silence and understanding silence as a text with a variety of students and professionals working in education. This has been essential throughout my practice as a teacher educator as silence has been linked to disability in ways that are deficit-focused. Yet, students with disabilities who have been deemed "non-verbal' use silence in a variety of ways to communicate powerfully and clearly. Therefore understanding silence as a text and fostering literacy about silence has also been an important undertaking in my work as a researcher (Iannacci, 2008). Silence is a text and as such, can and should also be taught. Teaching silence as a text contributes to expanding understandings beyond current deficit conceptualizations of silence (Granger, 2003). This knowledge is integral for educators to develop in understanding and working with students who have disabilities that challenge their verbal production.

The whole-part-whole model was and continues to be a pedagogical frame that has helped ensure that context remains at the forefront of instruction. Direct and explicit part-focused teaching is important but follows and is used to support meaning-making rather than something done in isolation. Further and most importantly, students are enabled to use what they have been taught in order to demonstrate their understating of and ability to create the very texts that they are interested in, challenged by, or required to understand. What must be pointed out is that the time spent on each component of the whole-part-whole model varies. As such, there is not a set number of texts or lessons that can identify how long or what students will need to become immersed in and familiar with a type of text. Similarly, the number of parts in a text and how long these parts will take to teach is not universal or quantifiable. The number of lessons and time students will need to transfer what they have come to know about the parts in order to understand or create texts themselves will of course also vary. The point is to shift thinking away from conventional understanding of how instruction is configured (e.g., lessons, units, modules) in order to consider what learning processes require and how learning happens. Much damage has been done in education as a result of imposition and restriction of time. Standardizing and compartmentalizing learning has been harmful to many students. However, students with disabilities have been further maligned by constraints that are a result of regimented and routinized ways in which instruction has been configured in response to and as a result of how it occurs and is organized in institutions and as a result of standardization. An individual educational plan and identification processes that determine disabilities, placements and programing are more than enough reason to understand the needs of the student deemed "disabled" as requiring learning opportunities that are respectful of and responsive to their assets, interests, needs, and challenges. The whole-part-whole model is one way to organize instruction so that their learning remains the focus of what they are offered in education as opposed to schoolified rituals that disable and are disabling. The model can help foster and facilitate asset-oriented, multiliteracies-focused inclusive learning environments. These environments and the conditions and practices that help forward them are discussed further in the next section.

# CONDITIONS THAT SUPPORT MULTILITERACIES, ASSET-ORIENTED INCLUSIVE LEARNING ENVIRONMENTS

It is important to understand that developing a multiliteracies-informed, asset-oriented inclusive learning environment isn't prescriptive or accomplished by adhering to a list of strategies or practices. There are, however, conditions that have been identified as integral to learning that are relevant and applicable in reconceptualizing how disability and students with disabilities are understood and responded to within education. These conditions have been established and researched for many years by Brian Cambourne (1995, 2000, 2001, 2002) in an effort to understand what students do and require from teachers/learning environments in order to learn. The conditions and practices associated with these conditions will be defined and identified (Box 4.3) in order to provide a frame that can be used to help organize and forward learning environments that are responsive to and respectful of students with disabilities. Questions educators can consider in assessing the presence of these conditions in their classrooms are also offered.

---

**Box 4.3**

---

### Immersion

Students with disabilities need to be immersed in a variety of multimodal texts that enable, access, and develop literacies. Learning environments use a variety of communication options to ensure that students with disabilities are positioned and understood as asset-oriented (Heydon & Iannacci, 2008). Practices include people-first language, speech recognition software, environmental print supported by visuals and objects, recorded audio texts, reading that is teacher-led, done as a group, in pairs or individually, communication and sensory boards, and various types of assistive technologies geared towards learners' needs.

- Is my language and the language used in my classroom asset-oriented and focused on personhood?
- Are my students surrounded by and able to access a variety of technologies and multimodal texts?
- Am I providing learning opportunities that allow my students to become familiar with, understand, and use/create a variety of texts based on their assets and needs?


### Demonstration

Students need opportunities to observe and become involved in modelling the ways in which various texts and communication options are used and therefore become engaged in making explicit the features of texts and processes of learning. Practices include one-on-one instruction, video-recorded mini-lessons that can be viewed by learners repeatedly, providing concrete examples and exemplars, multi-sensory instruction, student-led demonstrations, and modeling.

- Am I providing my students engaging demonstrations that make what is being learned explicit?
- Do the demonstrations take on a variety of forms and use a variety of modalities?
- Are my students involved in these demonstrations?

## Expectation

Students with disabilities need to be in an environment where adults understand the assets they bring to the classroom and believe they are capable of acquiring others. Practices include accommodations and modifications, homogeneous and hetero-geneous groupings, a variety of placement options that may include withdrawal, expectations that are respectful and responsive to students' with disabilities zone of proximal development, processes of learning as the focus of instruction rather than curriculum coverage or schoolified rituals organized around time, and an under-standing of a student's disability as epistemology and identity rather than a list of universal deficits.

- Do I think of my students in asset-oriented ways?
- Have I have designed individualized instruction to ensure their success?

## Responsibility

Students with disabilities are provided opportunities to make learning decisions that facilitate ownership, independence, and agency. They are understood and treated as agentive and capable of making choices. Practices include providing them with learning options, using universal design (UD), differentiated instruction (DI) focused on their assets and interests, assigning them responsibilities and tasks based on their assets, interests, and abilities, self and peer assessment and instruction, and making provisions for students to demonstrate their learning in multiple ways that they have decided upon.

- Are my students provided opportunities to make decisions about their learning?
- Have I offered them a variety of choices?
- Are these choices reflective of their assets and multimodal?

## Approximation

Students with disabilities need to be able to have their learning attempts and hypoth-eses respected and validated. Practices include accepting and encouraging their processes and the work they produce as they are learning, providing them with opportunities to share what they are working on with others, encouraging them to take risks, demonstrating your own approximations and processes as you are teaching, viewing students' work through an asset-oriented lens that is focused on and makes explicit the learners' strengths and next steps.

- Do I value my students' learning attempts?
- Have I demonstrated and celebrated learning hypotheses?
- Have I provided opportunities for my students to take risks and the support to extend their learning?

## Employment (Use)

Students with disabilities need to be able to transfer and/or use what they know and have learned in ways that are authentic, meaningful, purposeful, and useful. Practices include having them create texts after they have been immersed in them and understand their features, real world problem solving scenarios and activities, large blocks of time to gain an understanding of and ability to create a variety of multimodal texts, learning conferences with students that are asset-oriented and goal-focused, instructional level materials that are age appropriate and geared toward their interests and challenges.

- Have I provided my students opportunities to use what they have learned in meaningful ways?
- Are my students able to demonstrate their learning in a variety of modalities?

## Response

Students with disabilities need to receive asset-oriented and goal-focused feedback. Assessment and evaluation used to generate this feedback needs to be meaningful and responsive to their literacies and epistemologies. Practices including feedback can be provided by a variety of people who understand what multiple forms of assessment and evaluation can be and what demonstrations of knowledge can look like and mean, using a variety of formative and summative assessment tools and tracking devices, modeling asset-oriented feedback to peers and other students working with students with special needs and celebrating and sharing the students' work and accomplishments in a variety of modalities.

- Am I providing students with feedback that focuses on their assets and identifies a goal?
- Do I provide opportunities for students to assess their own learning and their peers' learning?
- Do I understand the various modalities that students use to demonstrate knowledge and have provided meaningful feedback that celebrates and furthers their work in that modality?

### Engagement

This condition is central to and embedded within each of the conditions. Students with disabilities need to see themselves as valued and valuable members of learning environments that are pedagogically engaging and responsive to their assets and needs. This provides them with powerful reasons to invest in and feel a part of their learning. Practices include respecting and accessing their prior experiences and knowledge, providing them with opportunities to engage with high-interest multimodal texts and topics, ensuring that learning materials provided for them are geared to their zone of proximal development and have utility, learning opportunities are real world–focused, personal, and useful, assessment and instruction is multimodal and respectful of their ways of knowing/ways of demonstrating their knowledge.

- Are students valued and valuable members of the learning environment?
- Am I providing students with an active, engaging, and asset-oriented learning environment?

Although the learning conditions that have been identified and described are important, it is essential for school boards, school structures, and leadership to facilitate these conditions to enable asset-oriented, multiliteracies-informed, inclusive learning environments to develop. These important actors must therefore be discussed as they are crucial in bringing to fruition what has been explored throughout this book. Importantly, a reconceptualized understanding of inclusion requires administering, planning, preparing, and support. Ongoing professional development and collaboration among various professionals engaged in supporting inclusion is vital to its success. Currently many of the practices in systems work against facilitating this form of inclusion. Fraser & Shields (2010) note, for example, that when teachers do not feel equipped to implement inclusion, support staff such as educational assistants are left solely responsible for students with disabilities. To be clear, educational assistants are not in and of themselves either an accommodation or a signifier of inclusion. This is also true of resource rooms. Teachers therefore require the necessary support to develop accommodations in response to students' needs or co-develop them with members of a team focused on supporting a student. As such, team members share their knowledge of programming and curriculum that is reflective of and responsive to a student's zone of proximal development (Vygotsky, 1978). As noted previously, this means identifying programming and/or focusing on curriculum expectations that are just beyond a student's independent capabilities.

An educator's role is therefore pivotal in identifying and designing curriculum and accommodations students require to engage with and achieve these expectations. Educators foster inclusion by creating a learning environment that enables students to thrive. In order to provide such an environment, educators need support to understand and respond to the student's assets, interests, and needs rather than depending on a placement or resource (human or otherwise) to deliver the illusion of inclusion. Authentic, successful practices that foster inclusion therefore need to involve teachers, parents, assigned support staff, and leadership from administrators for planning and decision making. Schools and school boards need to develop effective plans and implement the required supports and services including ongoing professional development and opportunities for conversation, consulting, and the co-creation of planning and pedagogy in order for inclusion to occur.

Harpell and Andrews (2010) have identified differentiated instruction and a team approach as essential components for educational leaders attempting to systematically plan for and provide educators opportunities to operationalize inclusion. These authors argue that these vital components help to create a school culture where educators feel empowered to foster inclusion/inclusive practices. Similarly, Obiakor et al. (2012) argue that "inclusion for students with disabilities is most effective when teachers are collaborative and consultative" (p. 482). These authors identify various strategies that can structure this collaboration and allow it to occur. What the authors outline can enable a teacher to (1) provide instruction while another teacher provides students additional support, (2) group[6] students and have teachers work with specific groups, (3) allow teachers to plan together and teach a lesson to small groups, (4) have a teacher teach while another pre-teaches and re-teaches students who need additional support, and (5) create teaching teams that provide instruction in the same room and support students simultaneously (p. 483). This attention to professional development, collaboration, and multiple support models demonstrates that inclusion is neither a thing nor a place and it is not achieved by a single person. Rather, inclusion requires a collective response to ensure a community is valued, responded to, and provided for in ways that ensure its social and academic success. To provide this response, educational leaders working at various levels in schools and school boards must purposefully and thoughtfully organize opportunities for those working with students to discuss, design, and develop inclusive practices and environments. Although these particular professional practices are vital in forwarding inclusive learning environments, economic and structural factors also need to be considered in ensuring that inclusive spaces that are both pedagogically and ethically sound.

## SPECONOMICS AND THE ETHICS OF INCLUSION

Much debate has occurred about the economic costs of inclusion. Unfortunately, the discussions have created a problematic binary that unproductively focuses on whether inclusion is more or less expensive than previous models (Odom & Parrish, 2001). For example, the *Sharing Promising Practices Resource Guide: Kindergarten to Grade Four* (2010), published by the Ontario Psychological Association, reports that in one school board:

> Potential poor readers are being identified as early as kindergarten and provided with intervention through differentiated instruction in the classroom. This model means that children do not have to be removed from the classroom. . . . This model is thus cheaper to implement (after teacher in-service). . . . (p. 100)

In addition to the problematic practice of early intervention, our responses to learners with disabilities can no longer be organized and framed in this economic and crude manner under the guise of inclusion. These types of statements fail to consider how this "less expensive/more expensive" binary compromises and ignores the ethics of inclusion. Warnock (2010), a pioneer of the inclusion movement, has stated that inclusion was originally conceptualized on the grounds of its educational merit rather than its costs. In order for inclusion to be managed respectfully, effectively, and as originally intended, resources need to be managed responsively and strategically rather than based on misguided objectives and monetary misnomers. Inclusion is a social justice issue, so when discussions about its efficacy are reduced to debates about whether it is a cost-saving measure or not, students with disabilities are once again dehumanized. These debates are especially important as the economics of special education (speconomics) already positions students with disabilities as financially lucrative.

Iannacci, Muia, & Porco (2018) have noted that arguments that support labeling and categorizing structures position students with disabilities as requiring resources that only formal identification processes can secure. Disability therefore becomes something that must is officiated in order for institutional responses and resources to be allocated to a student who has been identified as disabled. This argument, however, conceals how systems create the "hunt for disability" (Baker, 2002) perpetuated by the lure of special education funding and the belief that resources can and will provide the necessary "treatments" to help "fix" disabled students. These resources (both human and material) benefit particular groups and organizations and need to be questioned as current special education systems and processes have configured pathologizing as necessary in securing these resources, thus preventing a critical consideration of the ethics of special education funding. Warnock (2010) reports that the committee of which she was part that originally advocated for inclusion "never thought that . . . children's supposed special needs would be exaggerated and exploited in order to attract more money for schools" (p. 1–2). We therefore need to reject pathologization and focus on ensuring that resources are sought based on students' needs rather than on attributing deficits to students in order to receive additional funding.

Iannacci, Muia, & Porco (2018) have also pointed out that in the current education paradigm, accounting measures perpetuate conceptualizations of exceptional students as "less than" or "faulty" because the allocation of resources is a numbers-driven process. In Ontario, for example, the reports that secure funding are submitted thrice yearly to the Ministry of Education.[7] The problematic and imprecise standards of testing and the subjective diagnostic descriptions and rating scales used to identify disability and to secure resources perpetuate the hunt for disability. Further, this hunt fosters a culture in which, in order to receive these resources, administrators, special educators, psychologists and consultants may find themselves unwittingly and unintentionally complicit in ensuring that these standards/criteria are met. This type of culture can create levels of disability that do not represent students' needs and a climate where students with disabilities are "used as pawns in a financial game" (Warnock, 2010). Further, this culture inaccurately and inappropriately diagnoses and perpetuates demographics that overburden systems and therefore perpetuate the argument that inclusion is unsustainable rather than focusing on a system that requires and rewards the pathologization of students. This issue raises critical questions about the ethics of understanding inclusion to mean only placing students with disabilities in regular classrooms in our current standardized-focused educational context after we have gone through great lengths to identify their specific needs and challenges that secures funding that is supposedly to be used to support them. All of the above requires a model of inclusion focused on to whom education and educators are ethically accountable rather than financial pursuits and polemics. This is essential in ensuring that the spedcycle is broken (see Figure 4.5) and that inclusion remains focused on forwarding social justice-oriented pedagogies and practices.

**Figure 4.5.    Breaking the Spedcycle**

**NOTES**

1. Chapter five will extend the conversation to parents who have children with disabilities and their experiences with education systems and support agencies.

2. The last section of this chapter provides more information about the economics of disability "speconomics" within education and develops a frame of ethical praxis in response to these economics.

3. This section on the cueing systems and their implications for instruction and assessment in relation to students with disabilities draws on and applies important contributions Ken and Yetta Goodman, David and Yvonne Freeman, and Marie Clay have made to understandings about literacy and literacy instruction. The author would like to acknowledge their seminal bodies of work.

4. The sequence of the *Jolly Phonics* timetable (e.g., week one: s, a, t, i, p, n) is organized so that "letter sounds are introduced at the rate of one letter sound a day" so that "all of the 42 letter sounds are...covered after about 9 weeks" (Lloyd, 1998, pp. 10–11). However, I have observed that the amount of time spent on each letter is usually much longer than a day and drawn out particularly when used to teach students deemed deficient (Iannacci, 2005).

5. Culturally and linguistically diverse students and students from low socio-economic backgrounds, for example (Barone, 2002; Delpit, 2003; Iannacci 2005; Iannacci in 2018).

6. Within inclusive learning environments, groups can be organized homogeneously or heterogeneously in terms of ability but can also can be formed based on students' similar assets and interests. Groups should be created and re-created fluidly and responsively.

7. See for example the *Special Education Funding Guidelines: Special Incidence Portion (SIP)*, 2015–2016.

# Chapter Five

# Parents of Students with Disabilities

This chapter provides educators and workers in community agencies at all levels opportunities to understand parental perspectives with respect to their children, their child's disability, and their experiences with education and related systems. Throughout my career in education I have simultaneously been struck by both the importance of parents and the ways in which they have been problematically configured in education. This has been especially the case with respect to parents of children with disabilities. The ways in which they are positioned and the lack of attention given to their voices has been an ongoing concern. Although relationships with parents are discursively understood as important within education and their role is depicted as that of a partner, there are often contradictions between idealized school-parent partnerships and actual practice. The story which follows, *Sitting Silent*, represents an amalgam of both personal experiences and those to which I have been privy over my twenty-five-year career in education. As you read through the story think about the ways in which parents are portrayed in the system and consider the implications of such a portrayal for the child and for you as an educator or community agency worker.

## SITTING SILENT

Mr. and Mrs. Naser were pleased with the progress their son Victor had made in Mrs. Danielle's self-contained special education class. They noticed that he was happy, had made a great deal of progress, learned many social skills, and had begun to make good friends. For the first time in his life he had even been invited to a birthday party. Victor was gentle, observant, and inquisitive and although born with physical and cognitive disabilities that presented daily challenges, he was happy to come to school and especially interested in math and writing poems. As Victor was now in grade eight, Mrs. Danielle, his special education teacher, had to prepare a transition plan for him so that the high school he would be attending in September would be able to successfully prepare for and respond to his needs. This mandatory process and planning meant that a formal meeting near the end of the school year at the board office would have to occur. Relevant faculty from Victor's new school, Victor's parents, Mrs. Danielle and a designated meeting chair would attend. The meeting was to solidify the transition plan and ensure that all of the paper work, parental permissions, placements and processes required for Victor to continue to have necessary supports would occur throughout his years in high school.

When Mrs. Danielle explained the nature of the meeting to Victor's parents, they had many reservations. Mr. and Mrs. Naser had immigrated to Canada in part due to the ways in which Victor's disabilities were misunderstood in their country. They told Mrs. Danielle that Victor had been physically abused by a teacher in their home country as the teacher believed Victor was "lazy" and "faking" the physical symptoms he frequently displayed as a result of the his disabilities. When they immigrated to Canada they were both elated by the supports Victor received in school but also uneasy and uncertain of the myriad of decisions and requests that the school system would make and require of them. They were therefore wary of the meeting and anxious about Victor's transition to high school. They had many questions they wanted to ask about all of the paperwork and forms they were required to fill out. They wondered what all this would mean for Victor in high school. On numerous occasions Mrs. Danielle had answered as many questions as she could and assured them that they would indeed get a chance to ask or tell faculty representing Victor's future high school anything they wanted. She noted that it was standard procedure for parents to be invited to speak and ask questions during these meetings. Although this seemed to quell some of their anxieties, it was clear that Mr. and Mrs. Naser were concerned about Victor's future and about the ways in which he would be supported in high school and beyond.

On the day of the meeting, Mrs. Danielle headed to the board office early so that she could greet and make Mr. and Mrs. Naser comfortable in the assigned room. When they entered, she welcomed them warmly and reviewed what would typically occur at this type of meeting. She stressed that they would have an opportunity to speak and ask questions. Mr. and Mrs. Naser seemed nervous. At one point Mrs. Naser took food out of her bag for her husband and herself and offered some to Mrs. Danielle. Mr. and Mrs. Naser apologized for eating and explained that they had both left work early to attend the late afternoon meeting and that they hadn't eaten all day. Although

Mrs. Danielle was also hungry, she declined and was embarrassed that she had nothing to offer them.

When faculty from Victor's future high school arrived, Mrs. Danielle introduced them to Mr. and Mrs. Naser. They spoke informally albeit awkwardly as they waited for the meeting chair to arrive.

After 15 minutes, Mrs. Danielle began to worry about whether the chair would arrive, then suddenly she entered the room and quickly sat down. The chair introduced herself and explained that she had just come from another meeting that had run late. Without further introductions, she began by briefly explaining the point of the meeting and what was to be accomplished by the end of it. The chair then asked Mrs. Danielle to give her report. Faculty from Victor's future high school were subsequently asked to speak about the supports Victor would receive starting in September which included a life skills class he would be enrolled in throughout his high school years.

Mr. and Mrs. Naser sat quietly and listened attentively. Although Mrs. Danielle had attended many of these meetings, she was struck both by the speed of the meeting and by how little was focused on Victor. Faculty from his new school did not ask a single question about him and the chair did not elicit these types of questions either. When the last faculty member finished speaking, the chair signed paperwork that was in front of her, handed the paperwork to Mrs. Danielle and asked that she get Mr. and Mrs. Naser to sign it after reviewing it with them. She then abruptly stood up, thanked everyone for attending and left the room. Mrs. Danielle was completely caught off guard and shocked by how quickly the meeting had ended. She was distraught that Mr. and Mrs. Naser were not given an opportunity to speak. She sank into her seat, unsure of what to do or say.

Faculty from Victor's new high school gathered their things, shook Mr. and Mrs. Naser's hands, and let them know they were looking forward to working with them and Victor. They then shook Mrs. Danielle's hand and thanked her for the information she provided. With that, they too left the room.

Mrs. Danielle was now alone in the room with Mr. and Mrs. Naser, who remained very quiet. Before going through the paperwork with them, she apologized profusely for what had just occurred and explained that she had never been to a meeting where the parents were not given an opportunity to speak. Although upset, she tried to remain calm and professional. She also assured them that she could set up a meeting with people from Victor's new school so that they could ask their questions and voice their concerns. Mr. and Mrs. Naser could see that Mrs. Danielle was uneasy and frustrated by what had happened. They politely assured her that they were fine and that they were "used to things like this happening." Mrs. Danielle then reviewed the paperwork with them and got their signatures. They told her how much they appreciated the work she had done with Victor, excused themselves, and left the room. Mrs. Danielle completed her own paperwork, walked out of the board office, and drove home.

Throughout her drive she replayed how quickly things went and wondered when she could have/should have interrupted the chair in order to ensure that Mr. and Mrs. Naser were given a chance to speak. She was angry with the chair, angry with the staff of Victor's new school, but mostly she was angry with herself. Every time she replayed the situation, all she could think of was Mr. and Mrs. Naser quietly sitting throughout the meeting with all of their concerns and questions, none of which were voiced. Under her breath she kept repeating their statement that they were "used to things like this happening" over and over again. She was determined to never have anything like that happen again and thought a great deal about what to do.

Shortly after the meeting with Mr. and Mrs. Naser, Mrs. Danielle met with the principal of her school to explain what had happened and to show him a mock agenda she had created for future meetings she would attend with parents. In the agenda she noted that after the chair's opening remarks, parents should be invited to speak next. She would also be sure to ask parents to share any information about their child if they so wished. After they spoke, their questions and concerns (if any) would be addressed and then all reports and formal paperwork would be distributed and managed. She also explained that she would place a framed photograph of the student they were discussing in the middle of the table so that all parties were reminded of the person they were speaking about and making decisions for. Further, whether the school paid for it or not, she would provide food for parents and participants during these meetings to create a more comfortable atmosphere. Mrs. Danielle's principal supported these practices and they were adopted on a school-wide basis. Mrs. Danielle began to participate in professional development and read research about parent/school relationships. She was even asked to conduct workshops on the topic. As Mrs. Danielle was a parent, she thought a great deal about Mr. and Mrs. Naser and how she would want schools to treat her if she had a child with a disability. What she had experienced had a significant, immediate, and long-term impact on her practice and understanding of parents with children who have disabilities.

## LITERATURE ANALYSIS

These experiences and the contradictions they illustrated between the discourse surrounding parent/school partnerships and the reality of them led me to conduct a literature review and analysis of special education texts written for educators that include information about parents who have a child or children with a disability. This literature analysis indicated that the scope of the information provided is limited and limiting. The texts I drew from tended to focus on informing educators about how parents should be managed rather than involvement in various special education processes (e.g., IPRC and IEP development). They stressed the importance of parental involvement but framed this as "training" for meetings and navigating systems. Although the literature acknowledged the idea that parents possess valuable knowledge about their children, it also cautioned educators to be suspicious of the limitations of this knowledge. The texts also identified the importance of educators explaining special education processes to parents and described ways to help educators help parents navigate special education systems and processes without ever discussing how to access what parents already know about these things and/or asking about their experiences with processes and systems. Instead the literature tends to focus on alerting educators to the mandates that dictate their relationships with parents and the rights of parents with children who have disabilities. There is also a plethora of strategies for managing parent-educator relationships together with tools and measures for gathering specific information from them. Some of the texts frame parents' experiences as predictable stages that mirror the grieving process. A common theme in the literature is offering advice to educators about how to understand and regulate parents' behavior by, for example, providing them with "tips" on how they can help their child be successful at school. None of the literature suggests accessing what parents know about their children and ways they ensure success with them at home.

The literature analysis ultimately revealed that parents were positioned as objects to be acted upon, deficient in understanding their child themselves and the special education system, in need of being informed by educators about their child's disability, as well as homogeneous in terms of their experiences regarding their child's disability. Overall, the information mostly served instrumental (getting things), regulatory (controlling behavior), and representational (transmitting information) language functions (Halliday, 1975) as it primarily focused on explaining what information to transmit and how to transmit this information in ways that get parents to do what educators/education systems want them to do. Halliday (1975) identified various functions of language and showed that the most common functions within classrooms emphasized a transmission model of knowledge (representational and regulatory) (Bainbridge & Heydon, 2017). It is therefore interesting that professional literature written for educators about their communication and relationships with parents also focus on and utilize these language functions.

Essentially, literature and information provided to educators about parents of children who have exceptionalities is often by and large focused on assimilating parents into institutional ways of knowing and being rather than on exploring their experiences as parents of a child with a disability.

Consequently, the personal and experiential funds of knowledge (FoK) (Moll, 1992) parents possess about their child and special education systems as a result of their experiences are largely ignored in the literature. Moll's FoK research contends that there are hidden and untapped home and community resources that schools do not recognize or draw on to inform curriculum, instruction, policy, or practice. His work challenges and disrupts the deficit model currently informing educator/parent/student interactions. Recognizing and understanding parent's funds of knowledge is therefore essential in assisting educators to support and respond to children with disabilities and their families in asset-oriented ways (Heydon & Iannacci, 2008). As you read through the case study that follows, once again think about the ways in which parents and children are portrayed and positioned and consider the implications of this portrayal and positioning in terms of your practice as an educator or community agency worker.

## RESEARCH: A CRITICAL CASE STUDY

My previous research and teaching experience validated the importance of providing educators at all levels and special education systems with opportunities to experience and understand parental perspectives in relation to their children with disabilities in order to inform education practice. I therefore wanted to further understand and document the experiences of parents with children with disabilities including their interactions with special education systems and community agencies. From this information, I wanted to identify the funds of knowledge they possessed about their child and their child's exceptionalities and the knowledge they acquired about special education systems/community agencies they have had to navigate throughout their child's life. This information would be ascertained in order to help educators and community agencies better understand, support, and respond to parents of children who have exceptionalities. I began conducting interviews with parents of children who have a disability/ies and in so doing it became abundantly clear that one case (Dan, Hannah and Tracey's story) not only mirrored what I had found in the literature analysis, but provided additional depth and significance to these findings. It was a story that in short, needed to be told and learned from. Methodologically, their story is presented as a case study (Yin, 2013) expressed as a critical narrative inquiry (CNI). Data that helped construct the case study provided in this chapter consists of three two-hour interviews over three years with Dan and Hannah about their child Tracey, who was officially diagnosed as having autism and a developmental disability. In addition to the interviews, Dan and Hannah provided 200 pages of important documentation that also helped tell their story. These multiple forms of data were used to construct the following case study which will be followed by a critical discussion and analysis of the central themes and relations of power present within it.

## DAN, HANNAH, AND TRACEY: THE EARLY YEARS

Dan and Hannah, a middle-class Caucasian couple introduce themselves as Tracey's parents during our first interview. They are well educated and hold graduate and bachelor degrees as well as professional credentials that have enabled them to work in education for many years. As we chat it becomes abundantly clear that Tracey's parents have both loved and been greatly challenged. They have endured many struggles because of the ways in which the world has responded to their daughter. In our early conversation, Dan and Hannah speak about how intuitive Tracey, now thirty, was in her early years. They mention both her sensitivity to her environment and the ways in which those around her feel.

> Hannah: She would *get it*. For years I would say she was my emotional barometer. If I walked into the house after work, she'd know where I was at emotionally, which is uncanny. There would be times she would come up to me, "Mom, sit and sing, please?" She would take me, she'd come right up, be persistent in my face, to come and sit and sing and we'd sit on the couch and intertwine our legs and we'd sing together or I'd maybe even play at the piano. She'd sit beside me and I would calm, she would calm. It was like she knew when I was stressed and needed to sit and sing. And she'd have me sit and sing and all was well. It was like, oh my goodness, you know what I need and you demand it, face to face to come and sit and sing. It was just interesting that she could read that and it would change it for both of us.

Dan and Hannah go on to describe Tracey as enjoying being around family and as she grew up being very outgoing and wanting to frequently visit relatives. They speak too of her tremendous appetite and her eagerness to enjoy a variety of different foods.

Hannah had a healthy pregnancy and neither she nor Dan had a history of disability in their family. However, at seven weeks, Hannah experienced a spontaneous miscarriage of a suspected twin, Tracey's twin. A week following the spontaneous miscarriage, Hannah had a horrible flu. Later, they received a letter that suggested that there had been an impaired blood flow to the fetus (Tracey) when the twin aborted. However, no definitive explanation for what had occurred was ever determined. The very "last thing that occurred to them" when Tracey was born was a disability of any kind. At birth, all of her developmental scores were excellent. However, days after her birth she was slow to regulate her body temperature and slow to catch on in terms of feeding. Hannah describes her daughter as an "easy, easy baby. Too easy . . . as she wasn't connecting."

Early on when Tracey did not meet developmental milestones, concerns were raised by Dan, Hannah and family members. They were referred to a specialist and at six months Tracey received physiotherapy.

Although Dan and Hannah both resisted a label at this time (not that one was forthcoming by doctors who didn't actually know what was going on with Tracey), they soon recognized the importance of a label to be able to get supports for Tracey.

Dan and Hannah were sent to an institute for genetic testing/counseling. There they followed a series of medical appointments during which physicians sought an appropriate diagnosis. Dan recalls someone "freaking out" over the size of his big toe (which he had never thought was big) and then being told that they suspected "Rubinstein-Taybi syndrome." He recalls checking everybody in his family's big toe. Hannah recalls Dan's mother running away and putting socks on.

A couple of years later a pediatrician told them she "strongly" suspected Rett's syndrome, a degenerative malady. Concerned by this potential diagnosis (made within minutes of meeting Tracey), they sought out another specialist who immediately and angrily dismissed it. During this time other doctors told Dan and Hannah that Tracey wouldn't begin walking until she was eight years old. She started walking at two.

## TRACEY AT SCHOOL

Tracey attended a preschool part-time at which Hannah supervised and taught. Proximity to people was important to Tracey as she wanted to be near them and hold their hands. Tracey enjoyed preschool and mutual interaction with her classmates. In preschool and then in kindergarten her teachers connected with Tracey and set up environments where the children understood, responded to, and integrated Tracey into play and social situations. Tracey remained in these classrooms until age six. During these years, Tracey was diagnosed as having autism and a developmental disability.

Following the preschool and kindergarten, Tracey was transferred and bussed to a school where she attended a special needs self-contained classroom for two years until she was seven. This too was a positive experience and Tracey again connected with the teacher and support staff.

Next, she was placed in another special needs self-contained classroom for primary age children where she and the teacher did not connect and the "high-strung" environment/teacher were not responsive to Tracey. Instead there was a focus on having Tracey "behave in a certain way," complete unmodified academic work, and sit for extended periods of time. This focus led to a "battle of wills" in which behaviors steadily escalated to the point where Tracey was screaming, spitting, scratching, and often was restrained. The school frequently called Dan and Hannah by 9:30 am, to ask them to pick Tracey up. Dan and Hannah felt that Tracey learned the negative behaviors during this time that she knew would result in her being removed from the classroom where she didn't want to be and then being picked up by her parents.

Dan and Hannah describe that the school framed everything about Tracey as a "problem, problem, problem." Since Tracey was sensitive to her environment and emotions around her, tone of voice and energy in the room exacerbated her reactions. Tracey can "tell very quickly if someone doesn't like her" and in this school environment it proved very problematic.

Eventually, Dan and Hannah were called in every day to pick up Tracey. They felt "guilty" and "bad," as though they were "naughty," as if their child was a "reflection of them." They too felt as if they were a "problem."

Hannah: Even the comment from the principal saying, "Well, if my children are sick, I pick them up. That's what a good parent will do. That's what parenting is about. If your child needs you, you get them. So how is this any different?"

Dan: I would pick up a real attitude of condescension. I felt that many times we were spoken down to.

Hannah: Hey, you guys are the parents. This is *your* kid. Don't send us a kid who is going to yell and scream and misbehave and scratch and spit. Fix her before she comes.

Dan: In other words, train her before you send her to school.

The principal validated calling them every day to pick up Tracey by referring to the "zero tolerance policy" that was quite dominant and applied universally and incorrectly at this time.

Hannah: I was a problem because I did not like the idea of having to be called at any given time of the day, week to come and pick her up *immediately* because they were not able to manage. I really believed she needed the socialization. I felt that she had a right to be in school in a classroom.

Community agency personnel became involved at this juncture and informed Dan and Hannah that the school was not providing the legally minimal amount of time required for Tracey. Although Dan and Hannah began resisting the school's requests to pick Tracey up, the school continued to assert this practice, perhaps even creating conditions for making such calls.

Dan: So, by us starting to resist a little bit being called every day, we weren't being good parents.

Hannah: "We expect you to be here in 15 minutes" (quoting the principal in a stern tone).

Dan: We both had full-time jobs.

Hannah: It was a lot of pressure and sometimes I kind of wondered if, when they took her out of the taxi or the bus, whichever it was, if they might have just antagonized her just so that they could make the call. I don't know. Sometimes you kind of wonder do they set her up for this?

Dan and Hannah were highly pressured to put Tracey on medication at this time to control her behaviors. They went through many trial errors and at times were afraid for her life as she showed signs of overdose. No amount of medications altered the behaviors and they remained desperate to try anything for Tracey to be successful in school.

Tracey was eventually transferred to a school specializing in students with disabilities. This move was immediately successful. The teacher, who had been given all of the information about Tracey's behavior in the previous classroom/environment, questioned and was puzzled by the problems the previous school had documented. She saw no trace of what had been described and loved having Tracey in the class. Tracey remained in the class for the next two years when a change in staff and classrooms occurred. This change unfortunately brought about the same behaviors exhibited prior to this successful environment.

At this time, medication was explored again and a low dose was decided on. Dan and Hannah hoped that this would show the school that they cooperative in trying to find solutions. Dan and Hannah, however, knew that the medications would not "fix" autism and it was clear to them that the most powerful factor in responding to Tracey's behaviors was a supportive environment and positive relationships. Unfortunately, the new context, like the previous unsuccessful one was "rigid," "forceful," and "prescriptive" and Tracey resisted. Dan and Hannah began "reliving" their previous experience.

Friends of Dan and Hannah who both held doctorate degrees, worked in educational systems most of their lives, and who also had a child with a disability offered to accompany them to a school meeting to advocate on their behalf. These friends were successful in articulating Tracey's needs and rights to the school. After the meeting there was a marked improvement in the situation.

Eventually the specialized school closed and Tracey, at fourteen, was sent to a secondary school special needs self-contained class. Associate families who shared personal and professional experience and the credentials for working with children like Tracey, were organized to provide some respite care and support for her. The associate families who also knew their rights as well as Tracey's, articulated these to the school when they felt they were infringed.

Although things were generally good and worked well during these years, the pattern of things going well in one classroom with one teacher and then not well when Tracey was assigned a different teacher/classroom continued. The same issues prevailed. When the environment and teacher were flexible and responsive, Tracey genuinely felt liked and things went well. When the opposite was true, Tracey resisted and reacted. However, with the help of associate families, the schools Tracey attended were much more responsive and aware of their responsibilities and quicker to make changes to accommodate her.

## TRANSITIONING OUT OF SCHOOL: CREATING A CRISIS

At 21, Tracey was required to leave high school. Funding for Tracey and her supports were in transition at this age.[1] Bureaucratically it was a pivotal year that Dan describes as a time when "all hell broke loose." No longer eligible to attend school, Tracey needed a day program, outings, and an adult living arrangement. In an effort to provide her with all of this, her case worker at the time believed that getting Tracey a dual diagnosis of autism/schizophrenia would better position her for these necessary supports. This "strategy" proved "successful" for both the case worker and her agency. Dan and Hannah knew nothing of the "create a crisis" strategy as it was never explained to them initially. They would never have agreed to it as they did not believe Tracey was schizophrenic "for a minute." Tracey's associate family was, however, aware of and supported this strategy and the attempted dual diagnosis.

Tracey was placed on increased medication, which Dan and Hannah felt was a result of stressors introduced in the associate family's home at the time. She had a paradoxical reaction to this medication and became increasingly anxious and aggressive. Several times over a three-week period Tracey had an outburst and was rushed to the hospital, restrained, made a ward of the hospital, placed in the psych ward, and heavily medicated with powerful psychotropic drugs.

> Dan: We get a call from the hospital that Tracey had been admitted. We knew exactly what had transpired. She had a temper tantrum at home which . . . they were becoming more frequent and so they called the hospital, ambulance came, picked her up, and took her in. She was fine. Apparently, from what I hear she was sitting in the waiting room and she was quite content; she was quite happy.

But when they tried to take her into an examining room, she was afraid and so she resisted. And you know . . . a toddler mentality in a 21 year old body, she did what she could. She resisted, lay down on the floor, started screaming and fighting people off of her and so immediately she was now admitted on this Form 4 and placed into 5 point restraint. This lasted for a total of three weeks and she ended up on 7 point restraint, on medication . . . Olanzapine, all kinds of drugs, extremely powerful psychotropic drugs that she had never been on. They were using medication as a strait jacket. And trying to talk to the staff . . . you may as well just throw yourself off of a high tower.

Hannah: I think one of the pieces in wanting to help Tracey and do better for her was to get her on medication that would just calm her emotional behavior.

Dan: A magic pill, so-to-speak, which doesn't exist.

Hannah: It was often said, "What's the magic pill? Where's the magic pill? There's got to be something that's going to just take the edge right off her behavior."

The steady increase of medication ensured both physical and psychological trauma that Dan and Hannah tried to document by taking photos but were chastised for doing so. Hospital staff said their actions were "violating patient confidentiality and privacy." When Dan and Hannah contacted the media, health networks, and local politicians for help, some changes were made and they were able to take Tracey out of the hospital for three-day periods before a transfer to a facility was made available. The first attempt to take Tracey home for an overnight stay was unsuccessful. At this point Tracey was not eating, had a high temperature, was dizzy, couldn't stand up, and would fall. She was also panicked and couldn't sleep. Dan and Hannah feared for her life and demanded that the medication that they clearly thought was the cause of her rapid decline be stopped. Eventually the hospital cyclically complied and diminished her medication by each Friday so that Dan and Hannah could pick Tracey up for weekends. There was a marked improvement each time she was removed from medication. She went from breaking two beds while on medication to being returned to the hospital after the allowed number of days, sitting cross-legged waiting for a doctor to see her back at the hospital. The doctor was amazed at the difference. Nurses couldn't believe how Tracey thrived without medication. When Hannah was permitted to stay overnight with Tracey at the hospital, Tracey started to eat, walk, and communicate again.

Tracey was finally transferred to a mental health hospital for drug stabilization and assessment. The schizophrenia/autism dual diagnosis never occurred as Tracey was not deemed to be so by a variety of experts. She stayed in the mental health hospital for 11 months, during which time there was little or no meaningful human interaction for her. Tracey was put on a cocktail of drugs. She was down to 80 pounds during her stay, lost her speech and was no longer able to manage her own toileting. She would be left sitting cross-legged in a chair all day. She was periodically restrained during this time but not as frequently as while hospitalized. She was heavily medicated, but Dan and Hannah were allowed to take her out of this center on weekends.

Hannah: She was out a lot of weekends. Pretty well most weekends.

Dan: Yeah, she was out a lot of weekends. We hated bringing her back . . . hated.

Hannah: Because to take her back in after a weekend out . . . and she was very very quiet . . . it was a chore to get her to eat because the meds took her appetite. But for her to go back in, I felt like I was abandoning my child every single time. And putting her into abandonment. Torture. Often when we'd approach the center, Tracey would say, "No, no, no!"

Dan: By the time the eleven months was up, it was absolutely a case of failure to thrive. I think she would have gotten sick and died if she remained there.

Hannah: I asked, "What are you going to do if she continues to lose weight and she's not eating?" "Ah, we'll stomach feed her." A person, who all her life could eat like a horse, not gain weight because she didn't have all this medicine, she wasn't eating. There was no enjoyment of life anywhere, no connection to people.

After eleven months at the center (six months longer than the amount of time that is permitted at this center), a treatment bed with a community agency nearby became available. None of the treatment objectives and goals were met during her stay at the center, In fact she had regressed significantly.

Dan and Hannah continued to advocate for Tracey's removal from most of the medications in the mental health hospital. They brought in experts to help them make the case to do so but to no avail. Programming was also non-existent. Because she was not aggressive, Dan and Hannah articulated how what Tracey required at that point was a "permanent adult living situation."

Dan: We want to see her in a reasonable home in her home community where we can have some input into her day-to-day existence, where she can be part of her family because she likes that and she needs that. . . . She has been at the treatment center for three years. The center believes that it could take another two years to find Tracey a community living placement. . . . We need to see the final chapter. We need to see this come to a reasonable conclusion. Tracey needs to be now in a permanent place where we can say: This is her home. This is her home.

Hannah: We'd love it in the community so we could see her frequently through the week and on weekends. But if not, at least a home that is going to be able to have expertise as to where her needs are at, like an autism focus type of a place that just understands what her needs would be, and are willing . . . relationship, emotional support, reduced anxiety, a comfortable environment, that would understand her needs and meet those. Our goal for Tracey is no different than for any child that we would have had. We want her to be in a happy state of mind, in a caring place, community, with a life worth living.

Tracey remained in the treatment center for three years. Because the center was far from where Dan and Hannah live, they had an appointment with a community living agency a few days after our first interview. They wanted her placed in community living nearby and were concerned that the treatment center would prevent that from happening as it received substantial funding for Tracey. They had hopes and aspirations for their daughter but were concerned and suspicious that her current context may prevent her from getting what they wanted for her.

## DRUGS, FUNDING, AND FEAR

Dan and Hannah recounted that shortly after our first interview, the treatment center met with them a few times to discuss Tracey and their goal for her to have a community living placement within the vicinity in which they live so they could visit her. Their goal never transpired. Instead, the treatment center called them and declared that a permanent bed in their facility was available and that they would have to decide within six hours whether to agree to this placement. Forced with a tough decision and faced with no other available options, Dan and Hannah agreed that Tracey remain at the treatment center, although they were conflicted by the decision.

> Hannah: We debated and debated and debated and felt, how do we say no to something that is, we already know, for something that might not be, and are we trading some of our frustrations at the place at present for what might be frustrations at another place as well? Like is any place perfect?
>
> Dan: The devil that you know.
>
> Hannah: Or the devil that you don't know.

There were, however, changes in the staff at the center and how they related to Tracey. Also, the placement was not just a bed as Tracey was given her own room. This made the placement decision eventually less difficult for Dan and Hannah.

Hannah: The staff in there are wonderful with her. They seem to really care. . . *many* of the staff are really good with her and she's connected with them so that is good. Some of the things that we are most frustrated with are above that.

Tracey's loss of day to day skills was still apparent post the litany of psychotropic drugs she was on. Toileting and communication were still not at the level they once were nor was her interest in people, her emotional intuitiveness, or her activity. Dan and Hannah described her as "disengaged." Programming remained an issue. There were infrequent outings planned for her (e.g. walks, car rides). The institution suggested they did not have the staff to support more programming for her. Dan and Hannah tried many times to get a line by line accounting of how funding for Tracey was being spent but did not receive this information by the time of the second interview; they felt that the funding provided for Tracey more than covered what could be possible for her in the way of programming. They also believed that invoices they were given and required to sign in order for the institute to be reimbursed by the government inflated the services she was actually receiving.

Hannah: Many of the outings that they even record is "going for a walk." A walk should be a standard thing for anybody because it's just a physical exercise outing. A walk should be standard every day. If you can't even get a walk in, if that's your outing, how small is your world? And they can't even do that (chuckle)! Sometimes they include a drive through at Tim Horton's. It's a drive through. She gets in the van, they pick up some coffees for others, and that's her hour outing. You don't have to hire an extra person to do a drive through at Tim Horton's.

Dan: So it's very obvious that there is a bit of double billing going on. They're double dipping.

They attempted to not sign and submit invoices so the center did not receive money. However, they feared repercussions in doing so and were not sure how long to do so or how to proceed.

Hannah: So, since the beginning of this fiscal year, April 1st, I have not submitted the two invoices that they've given (chuckling). Yikes! But I've been insisting and I've said many times, I need documentation. You've got the form, fill it out, I'll submit it when I get it. I've even told them: I have not submitted during the first three months because I haven't got that documentation yet. They submitted another one with only the invoice and basically that total, so many hours and a total. I haven't submitted that . . . I'm trying to think through how to do it because here's a delicate situation again. If I make too many waves, are they going to be upset with Tracey? In what way might it come back in a negative way on Tracey and on us if I push too hard? But I'm pushing, wanting to make the best for Tracey but I don't know if it might turn around and bite us. I just don't know.

Dan: And we're not acting independent. In the strictest confidentiality, the staff who works with her on a day-to-day basis is confirming our suspicions (about the inflated billing).

They also wonder what the repercussions of their actions may be for Tracey:

Dan: There is definitely a discrepancy between what is actually happening and what is being billed and the staff have expressed surprise when they see the amount that is being billed. I guess I feel kind of caught between a rock and a hard place here because I don't know if suddenly they can decide Tracey's behaviors are escalating so maybe she needs to go back to (says the name of previous center where she was overly medicated), you know. . .

Hannah: And that could kill her . . . I don't want to see her back on that (the medications) because I don't know if she'd recover again, even to the point that she has recovered now, which is not fully.

Dan: I'm afraid of retribution.

Dan and Hannah stress that they do, however, feel better about having Tracey at the center due to the staff.

Dan: I mean the staff are really good; we enjoy the staff. We have no beef or argument with any of the staff but when Tracey is basically sitting there behaving relatively well, why rock the boat? Leave her alone.

Hannah: Some staff really work at trying to get her out. Sometimes they have ideas for outings and then the agency just says: Nope. We can't do it.

The second interview ended with Dan and Hannah articulating their desire for further interactions and programming for Tracey in order to stimulate her in hope that she would regain some of the skills and assets she once possessed. When they had Tracey at home with them or out with family/at family functions, they saw some of her reemerging. They wanted that furthered purposefully at the center and therefore wanted more accountability from the center as to how it spends her funding. They were, however, cautious and afraid of pushing the center too hard as they feared repercussions.

## MEDICATION INDUCED COMA AND AFTERMATH

Dan and Hannah revealed that shortly after our second interview, Tracey unfortunately was hospitalized again after being overly medicated. Her behaviors escalated after the increased medication and PRN's (prescriptions as needed) were abused in order to control her behaviors which were triggered by medications she was actually being given. Medically and physically she was restrained and eventually went into a medication induced coma. She was intubated and remained this way for 10 days. Several tests showed no new reasons for her episodes. Medications were lessened throughout her stay and eventually Tracey came to and was released. She was shaky and demonstrated withdrawal-like behaviors. She had trouble moving and communicating. Once again her body had been through trauma. After five days, she began eating and the center started to add drugs to her food, although if she suspected pills in her food (e.g., ice cream) she'd spit them out. Not all attempts at adding medications to her food were detected and eventually Tracey was once again heavily medicated. Tracey's behaviors escalated showing once and for all that the drugs were the most likely triggers for the behaviors. Dan and Hannah were told they had the right to refuse the drugs and they exercised that right. Further, they began speaking to experts to apprise them of the situation. A doctor wrote a report and identified the paradoxical reaction Tracey had to the drugs as well as outlining a plan of action that included ensuring that the necessary reduction in drugs continued. Further, this doctor ensured any and all drugs she required would be reviewed for their actual effects/benefits and also be lessened or no longer prescribed based on this review.

Now a year after the coma, Tracey is on very few medications and doing much better. The new medical strategy with/for Tracey opposes the old strategy; that is, finally, how little medication can she be on, and whatever she is on is questioned and reviewed for its effectiveness and benefits. Dan and Hannah say that everyone "is in a good place right now" and that "things are good." However, as demonstrated by their story, they also believe that "it's never over, it's episodic. You just hope that if it goes south, it gets sorted faster."

## DISCUSSION AND IMPLICATIONS

Data from the story reveal discourses, processes, and coercive relations of power that prevented educators, schools, and community agencies from fully developing ethical, respectful, and reciprocal interactions and relationships with parents. A critical discussion of these findings provides the background for shifts in perspectives and practices that facilitate a reconceptualization of disability within education as it relates to people with special needs and their parents.

It was clear from the data that the forms of pathologization Tracey experienced were projected onto Dan and Hannah. Subsequently, powerful disability discourses and related practices extended and led to human rights violations and an unethical and problematic approach to funding. Pathologization has been defined as:

> . . . processes by which persons belonging to a particular group are seen by a more powerful group as abnormal in some way and this supposed abnormality is perceived as in need of fixing, usually through some sort of medical or scientific intervention. (Heydon & Iannacci, 2008, p. 4)

Shields, Bishop, and Mazawi (2005) similarly conceptualize pathologization as occurring when "perceived structural-functional, cultural, or epistemological deviation from an assumed normal state is ascribed to another group as a product of power relationships, whereby the less powerful group is deemed to be abnormal in some way" (p. x). It was clear that Dan and Hannah experienced pathologization almost immediately after Tracey was born. Results of genetic testing and the subsequent attempt to locate reasons for Tracey's disability demonstrated the ways in which disability has been problematically understood and organized within society. Although the "big toe" incident is absurdly funny, it reflects how disability is "nomenclature for a negative ontology and posed as a way of being that at all costs ought to be avoided" (Baker, 2002, p. 685). Dan's mother running away and hiding her toe in order for the location of disability to be determined as being a result of her genetics reveals how disability continues to be considered something shameful and to be hidden.

Pathologization was also evident in the ways in which Tracey's disability was described by the principal of Tracey's school as an illness that by extension, Dan and Hannah were responsible for and responsible for fixing/managing. The school's insistence that Dan and Hannah pick Tracey up from school on a constant basis and the violations of their rights as a result of this practice fully demonstrated the ways in which a school official (the principal) used power coercively and in ways that positioned Dan and Hannah as deficient and negligent. It was only after friends and community advocates who possessed lauded capital (e.g., their doctoral degrees) stepped in that the school altered its approach to Tracey, Dan, and Hannah in ways that were reflective of their rights. This speaks to the power of privilege and its impact on parent/school/community agency interactions. What must be noted is that Dan and Hannah's own social and cultural capital and privilege (i.e., educated, middle-class, English speaking, well networked) were definite factors in enabling this advocacy strategy. Interestingly, even with all of the capital they possessed, they experienced pathologization and immense challenges with the school. In fact, throughout interviews two and three it was difficult for Dan and Hannah to recognize their privilege given what they experienced. It is distressing to think about how parents who have much less capital than Dan and Hannah navigate the discourses, policies, processes, and relations of power they encounter. When this was pointed out to Dan and Hannah during interviews two and three, they had a great deal of empathy for these parents and specifically mentioned how difficult navigating systems and situations they encountered would be for parents who did not speak English. Mr. and Mrs. Naser are prime examples of the ways in which systems can silence parents who do not possess privileged forms of social cultural capital. This is especially troubling as the capital Dan and Hannah possessed literally made the difference between life and death for their daughter Tracey.

The case study also revealed significant tensions between restrictive and responsive environments for Dan, Hannah, and Tracey. It is essential to recognize that these tensions were not based on whether environments were regular classrooms or specialized environments. In other words, the conditions within the learning environments Tracey was exposed to either ensured or denied her success within them. By extension, Dan and Hannah faced enormous difficulties as a result of these conditions. Tracey's history in school does, however, mostly reveal that specialized environments were exceptionally helpful to her when her assets were respected and responded to appropriately. As such, her emotional intuitiveness, sensitivity, and need for physical contact were recognized and honored. When Tracey was not accommodated and positively responded to, she sensed and reacted negatively to the rigidity and animosity she encountered within these environments. As such, specialized environments where Tracey's emotional and physical needs remained the focus of programming for her created conditions that ensured that she thrived. We therefore need to recognize that the health and well-being of students like Tracey require us to create places within schools that ensure safety, care, and responsiveness to their assets and needs. This provision is at the heart of what inclusion is supposed to offer, and as such, provisions and placements that create this type of inclusive space must be understood as possible outside of the classroom and as needed by students within schools.

The case study ultimately demonstrates what Cummins (2001) terms coercive relations of power as so much of what occurred within it was focused on assimilating parents toward institutional ways of knowing and being rather than on exploring their assets (e.g., their experiences and what they know about their child) and the "special education maze" (Anderson, Chitwood & Hayden, 1997) they have had to navigate and negotiate. Data show the importance of providing educators and caregivers at all levels opportunities to understand parental perspectives in relation to children with special needs. This is precisely the type of information that is lacking in professional literature analyzed at the beginning of this chapter. This literature's coercive approach to relations of power with parents mirrors and supports Dan and Hannah's experiences with schools, community agencies, and institutions, as does what Mr. and Mrs. Naser experienced. As such, literature intended for educators and approaches to parents in education need to acknowledge, elicit, and respond to individual and idiosyncratic experiences parents have as well as recognize the vast amount of knowledge they possess about their children and systems they have had to navigate.

The most striking and problematic finding within Dan, Hannah, and Tracey's story is the similarity between asylum practices of the 1500s–1800s and current responses to people with disabilities. Throughout Tracey's experiences with schools, mental health facilities, and community agencies, the insatiable need to medicate as opposed to provide for her in ways that are responsive and reflective of her rights was both rampant and repugnant. The chemical restraints Tracey endured were no better than the physical restraints and torture techniques employed by asylums that we now denounce as inhumane. In both cases, these abusive practices stem from an inability to effectively provide for and respond to people with disabilities. In Tracey's case, this was even more evident after she turned twenty-one and no longer eligible to stay in school leading to serious and debilitating violations of her rights. On a larger scale, a lack of responsive provisions and human rights violations are further demonstrated in the overrepresentation of medicated and incarcerated youth who have disabilities and the "school-to-prison pipeline" (National Council on Disability, 2015) this has created.

Revealing these relations of power and the discourses that inform them enables a much needed shift in perspectives and practices that facilitate a reconceptualization of disability as it is configured in education. It is clear from the data there are a number of ineffective parent/school communication patterns and relations that prevent healthy and reciprocal partnerships between schools and parents from developing. As demonstrated by the case study, school interactions and communication have been judgmental and reflective of "dumping" (Curwin, 2012), which is a tendency to focus on a long list of deficits when speaking to parents about their children and then holding them solely responsible for "fixing" these problems. Dan and Hannah described this dumping as the school framing everything as a "problem, problem, problem" when speaking about Tracey and being condescending and aggressive in their insistence that they "fix" these problems. In the case of Dan, Hannah and Tracey, this "dumping" was also strategic in "creating a crisis" that the school used to achieve its goal of having Tracey picked up. Similarly, the community agency used this same strategy to try to receive more funding for Tracey. Whatever the motive, "dumping" in order to "create a crisis" is unethical, problematic, and in Tracey's case, life threatening.

Even when the "dumping to create a crisis" approach to students does not lead to a drug induced coma, it furthers student's pathologization which has a direct impact on their identity and life course options. When students are perpetually understood as a problem and unmanageable they see themselves as such and who they are as learners and people is absent in programming and placements that need to be developed and secured for them. Pushing them out of school as a result of failing to respond to their needs and absolving our responsibility to create learning opportunities for them because they reach a legal age where school is no longer responsible for them helps to ensure the proliferation of the school-to-couch and school-to-prison pipeline. Both of these pipelines are destructive, unacceptable, and must be broken.

Given the *Sitting Silent* narrative and Dan, Hannah, and Tracey's story it is more than evident that schools need to create healthy relationships with parents that are based on and build trust. As such, what must become a focus in communication and during interactions with parents is a concentrated effort to create opportunities for their voices to be heard and to listen intently to what they are saying. What they are offering must be understood as knowledge that they have learned about their child and the systems they have had to navigate. As such, the coerciveness that all too often impedes listening must be rejected in order to position parents as experts about their children and the experiences they have had while dealing with schools and agencies.

Although listening is imperative, educators must utilize parents' knowledge about their children in ways that inform programming and placements designed and assigned to students. As such, what must remain central in school/parent communication and interactions is the need to co-construct goals and approaches to achieving these goals for the child/student being discussed. Parents can provide valuable insights about their child's assets, interests, needs, and challenges. This knowledge is invaluable in creating responsive planning, programming, and informing placement decisions for the student. The level of co-constructed goal identification and approach to meeting goals requires communication that contradicts the instrumental, regulatory, and representational language use rampant in parent/school communication. Instead, educators need to begin to look for and document information parents have about their child and share what they have learned with the parents in order to verify the information and vet any decisions they have made. Communication must therefore occur regularly rather than when there is a "problem." To this end, communication can begin and end with what the educator/school has learned about the student insofar as their assets and interests and how this knowledge will be used to further develop programming that addresses challenges they are having. Parents can also be asked about their child's assets and interests and how they are capitalizing on them at home. The last part of meetings with parents can in fact be used to share successes they are having at home with their child as this information also provides insight into how they may be approached at school. In short, it is essential to avoid deficit-focused communication. Further, modes of communication have to be discussed and agreed to by the parent. It is therefore respectful and necessary to identify how, when and where to best reach parents to discuss their child. All of the information shared during meetings must also be documented and presented to the parents as a way of ensuring that what they have said has been understood. This documentation also demonstrates to the parents that what they have shared with the school is valued and valuable.

Given the difference in capital between Mr. and Mrs. Naser and Dan and Hannah, it is important to note that effective school/parent communication does not just consider sociocultural differences or is culturally sensitive. There is a need for awareness of how schools privilege certain types of capital parents possess (e.g., language, class, education), so that schools do not respond to parents in ways that are inequitable. It is therefore essential for schools and educators to be honest about the ways in which differences in parent capital are understood and responded to within education. Educators need to be cognizant of how differently they treat parents who possess privileged capital and compare their behavior to how they respond to parents without these forms of capital. Such critical questioning is necessary to understand and make visible the forms of inequity reinforced and furthered by these responses to capital within education. This type of critical questioning and reflexivity helps to shed light on the ways in which power differentials within schools mirror and maintain societal inequities. An awareness of and a destabilization of these communication patterns works to eradicate these inequities.

On a final note and one that is related but not entirely focused on parent/school communication, it is essential to address policies that essentially push students with disabilities out of school after they reach a certain age. Given the enormous number of school closures, and the fact that parents are pulling their special needs children from resource starved schools (Bouevitch, 2016), it seems that this particular policy and practice is unresponsive, ineffective, and disadvantageous to public education. The entire role of public school in terms of people with disabilities therefore needs to be reconceptualized in ways that open possibilities to offering programs and programming to special needs leaners who "age out" of the system. Moving in this direction would not only address the school-to-couch pipeline but also increase the purpose, value and strength of public schools as well as funding allocated for students who attend them.

The next and final chapter synthesizes the previous five chapters in order to clearly identify and define reconceptualized approaches to disability within the field of education. Practices, processes, and pedagogies will be brought together to provide the reader with a final overall schema for understanding and responding to disability in educational contexts in ways that facilitate a reconceptualization of current notions and practices.

## NOTE

1. The aftermath of this policy has created what has been termed the "school-to-couch pipeline" for students like Tracey.

# Chapter Six

# Summary

## *A Reconceptualized Approach to Disability in Education*

> It was a great satisfaction to learn and know more, it helped to ease one over a lot of puzzling matters . . . nevertheless, it brought, too, the first taste of complications from which we would never again be free. Quite quickly it became difficult always to remember how much one was supposed to know. It called for a lot of restraint to remain silent in the face of simple errors, to listen patiently to silly arguments based on misconceptions, to do a job in a customary way when one knew there was a better way . . .
>
> —*The Chrysalids*, John Wyndham, 1955

The process of reconceptualization is multifaceted and demands a shift in thinking and discourses combined with a transformation of pedagogy and practice that places ethics at its very core. The summary in this chapter is only useful when considered in conjunction with the exploration of each point in previous chapters. Thus, the chapter consolidates the contents of the book and provides an overview of the book's main points and perspectives.

## UNDERSTANDING OF SELF AND DISCOURSES THAT SHAPE DISABILITY

Stakeholders in education need to examine their own personal histories with disability/people with disabilities and therefore consider the ways in which this history intersects with and impacts their understandings of and responses to students with disabilities. Essential to this critical autographical process is the linking of personal histories and understandings of disabilities/people with disabilities to the dominant discourses that have shaped this history and these understandings. As discourses inform thoughts about and responses to disability and students with disabilities, educators need to critically interrogate these discourses in order to forward asset-oriented inclusive practices. Since historical conceptualizations of and dominant ideologies about disability continue to shape what we think about people with disabilities, educators need to be aware of and vigilant about destabilizing what exits at the macro level (society) as it has and continues to have an impact on what is occurring at the micro level (the classroom).

## NECESSARY SHIFTS

Reconceptualizing disability in education requires essential shifts in the ways in which society thinks and talks about disability and people with disabilities. As stated previously, how we think and talk about students with disabilities and how we respond to them are heavily linked. Educators therefore need to critically interrogate and reject the longstanding medical model that has been and continues to be dominant in education. This means that disability and people with disabilities must no longer be thought of as ill, inherently flawed, and in need of interventions that are supposed to "fix" them. Disability needs to be reconceptualized in ways that understand it as a socially constructed phenomenon and therefore, a placeholder for biases, misnomers, prejudices, and misconceptions. In short, what is required is a necessary shift away from the medical model to a social model of disability that is focused on how society renders disability pathological, rather than on hunting for and locating pathologies within people in order to eradicate it.

Our understandings of the social model of disability must additionally be informed by critical perspectives, specifically those developed in critical disability theory and research. These perspectives need to inform understandings of disability in order to elucidate the oppressive and inhumane ways in which people with disabilities have been understood and treated as a result of problematic and dominant discourses that have shaped and continue to shape how disability is taken up in society and by extension, schools. Education and educators need question the social construction of disability as well as ask who that construction serves and who and how it marginalizes. Such a shift in thinking needs to be reflected in language that we use in relation to, and assign to, disability/people with disabilities. This shift in language is not only facilitated by "people first" language but also by rejecting the dominant deficit model that continues to plague education in the ways in which students with disabilities are positioned and defined.

Institutional and institutionalized discourses and definitions of disability (e.g., those found in the DSM-V and other texts that draw from it) therefore need to be critically questioned and understood as artifacts of power as these disability categories are created by people in powerful positions who decide how disability will be defined. These definitions are presently deficit, and diagnoses-focused and very influential in organizing thought, language and practice in relation to disability/people with disabilities. The DSM-V and other texts that draw from it (e.g., school focused government texts that define disabilities) provide criteria that serves the "hunt for disability" (Baker, 2002), yet its content and categories has been both temporal and controversial. These texts can therefore no longer be viewed as infallible and determinate in their ability to officiate disability and provide stakeholders unquestioned and unquestionable criteria and diagnoses uncritically and without a sense of the socially constructed nature of their creation, revision and removal. If we are to read and write disability differently as Titchosky (2007) suggests, we need to view texts like the DSM-V and those that draw from it through a critical social justice lens. This fundamental shift must occur in order to ensure that education is personhood rather than pathology-focused.

In addition, education needs to embrace and become committed to an asset-oriented (Heydon & Iannacci, 2008) model of inclusion that positions students with disabilities as possessing valuable and valued funds of knowledge (Moll, 2005), resources, epistemologies, identities and legacies (Delpit, 2003). In short, disability needs to be considered an asset from which others can learn and benefit. Respect, responsiveness, relationship, and reciprocity are key to fostering this way of understanding disability in inclusive learning environments. Within these environments, asset-oriented language and perspectives can be taken up in ways that ensure that personhood is the focus of thinking about, talking about and being responsive to people with disabilities. Students with disabilities are then subsequently understood, spoken about, positioned, and provided for as "at promise" (Swadner & Lubeck, 1995) rather than "at risk."

## CRITICAL REFLEXIVITY

Narratives abound within the field of education and are potentially rich vehicles for critically interrogating practices, policies, and procedures that subjugate people with disabilities. Narratives provide educators opportunities to critically reflect on their practice or phenomenon they have observed or experienced. Linking these narratives to contextual and theoretical information and research allows for a variety of perspectives and alternative ways of seeing and being to emerge. As a result, educators have the potential to reconceptualize their practices and therefore education through this critical contextualization. Such a process is therefore not just about self-reflection, but rather reflexivity as educators become attuned to the ways in which the practices they examine are problematic and connected to a host of discourses, histories, and macro relations that have shaped and continue to shape education. It is a process that places the self in society in an effort to reveal structures and dynamics that create conditions that serve some while subjugating others. Awareness of these relationships fosters a heightened sense of context, culture, power, and resultant practices. This process also works against self-laceration and blaming as it is focused on explication of what is, deconstructing why it is, and then working toward what can be. The contextualization process is personal, powerful, and productive in its ability to enable a destabilization of taken for granted monoliths that continue to configure disability and people with disabilities in education in ways that are violative. Creating and critically reading narratives in order to reconceptualize education is ultimately an aesthetic, analytic, and ameliorative process focused on ethics.

## ETHICAL PRAXIS

Critical reflexivity and the reconceptualization of practice it can facilitate is integral to fostering ethical praxis, which is practice that is reflexive. This form of ethics is not about determining a singular "right" thing to do or the "right" way to do it, but rather making idiosyncratic decisions based on a critical interrogation of multiple and complex factors influencing specific situations. Ethical praxis is context-dependent, situated, and amorphous. It is also dependent upon an educator's critical awareness of his/her history, discourse, context, power, and practice. This knowledge is not rendered null and void each time a new situation presents itself that requires ethical navigation but rather becomes part of the repertoire of experiences and knowledge educators carry forward to inform and navigate new situations in ways that are sophisticated and when necessary, subversive. Ethical praxis is stalwart in its commitment to social justice and as such, requires a heightened awareness of inequities that continue to be reinforced within education. This critical awareness becomes the impetus for decision making and attempts to rally against, disrupt, and ultimately end inequities. Developing and focusing on ethical praxis is vital to an asset-oriented understanding of and approaches to disability and inclusion within education. It ultimately is focused on addressing the assets, interests, and challenges of students with disabilities rather than serving coercive systems and relations of power.

## RIGHTS AND ETHICAL RESPONSIBILITIES

Ethical praxis is especially evident when thinking about and making decisions for placements which students with disabilities may require and benefit from. It is essential to understand that inclusion is a legal right that requires a thoughtful consideration of placement options that respond to students' assets, interests, and challenges. A singular focus on placing students in general education classrooms under the illusion of inclusion does not conform or respond to the legal rights and ethical responsibilities education and educators have for students with disabilities. It is necessary to be suspicious of rhetoric, policy, initiatives, and mandates that declare inclusion as only being possible in the general education classroom. This stance is not only problematic, but can potentially thwart rights and resources students with disabilities are afforded and must have. A critical awareness is especially important given the ways in which standardized curriculum and evaluation continue to be dominant in education and detrimental for students with disabilities. Placement decisions therefore need to be informed by a plethora of factors that are foremost guided by a thorough understanding of who the student is, what their disability is, how their disability specifically has shaped their way of knowing and abilities, the quality of pedagogy and supports available at the school, and how well these supports are resourced and used. Placement decisions are therefore not made by default and under the delusion of inclusion, but rather by a careful, critical, and considered process that reconciles important factors that help determine what is in the best interest of the student rather than the system in which he/she or their teachers/parents are entrenched. In addition, fluid, malleable, and responsive placement decisions are altered and revised based on student assets, needs, and interests and not dependent upon or governed by bureaucracy.

## FROM LITERACY TO MULTILITERACIES

Standardized curriculum and evaluation practices ensure that limited demonstrations of print knowledge are privileged within schools. This privileging and the policies, pedagogies, and policing of schools it has fostered has compromised the rights of students with disabilities. Literacy has therefore been and continues to be a colonizing force in the lives of students with disabilities. The limited and limiting ways in which literacy has been configured to privilege print and verbal utterance has ensured that students with disabilities are understood as deficient or illiterate. This way of seeing them is dangerously intertwined with the denial of their personhood as print and talk have been and continue to be privileged signifiers of what it means to be human (Kliewer, Biklen and Kasa-Hendrickson (2006). As such, what is required of education and educators is a shift in understanding literacy as singular to one that recognizes and responds to the various ways in which people are literate. The multiliteracies people possess, can demonstrate, and use to make sense of and communicate their responses to and understandings of the world must be acknowledged and respected. Multiliteracies perspectives recognize and capitalize on the various ways people come to understand and demonstrate their knowledge of the world and how this occurs in various contexts through a variety of modalities. The various modalities that can facilitate meaning-making need to be made available and accessible to students with disabilities. Multiliteracies pedagogies can therefore facilitate universal design, differentiated instruction and the development of inclusive instruction.

A variety of semiotic systems and the sense-making processes students with disabilities access can therefore no longer be viewed through the same lens that dominates education at the expense of people with disabilities. As such, their multiliteracies must begin to be seen as necessary to access, foster, value, and further, to be in keeping with their legal rights and education's/ educators' ethical responsibility to them. Multiliteracies-focused pedagogies must therefore be offered to students with disabilities in order to create learning environments that are not just the "least restrictive," but rather the most responsive.

Importantly, multiliteracies pedagogies ensure that instruction is context rich and meaning-making-focused. Meaning-making processes are understood as requiring instruction that accesses the various resources (cueing systems) students use to make sense of texts in ways that are not print-dependent. Educators must therefore see all of the cueing systems as important resources students with disabilities use as they demonstrate their literacies while engaged in reading and creating a variety of multimodal texts. The whole-part-whole framework and specific conditions Cambourne has developed (1995, 2000, 2001, 2002) can be applied and used to help organize context-embedded, engaging, and responsive instruction for and with students with disabilities. These instructional frames and conditions are of course only effective when educators remain open to and focused on responding to learners' with disabilities assets, interests, and challenges.

## LEADERSHIP, STRUCTURES, AND FUNDING

Reconceptualizing disability in education depends upon leadership that facilitates consultative collaboration and provides opportunities for responsive professional development. These forms of collaboration see inclusion as supported by a variety of placement options and school personnel. As such, a student's needs and a school's response to these needs guides decision making and the allocation of required resources and staff. Professional development that facilitates this responsiveness is focused on a student's assets, interests, and challenges as opposed to deficit-oriented definitions of the student's disability and institutional and bureaucratic ways of managing the student's disability.

Discussions and decisions about the economics of inclusion and funding for students with disabilities need to be informed by ethical praxis in order to ensure that the personhood of students with disabilities is not compromised and that legitimate resources are accessed to identify and support their needs. Debates focused on whether or not inclusion is less or more expensive to deliver need to therefore be understood as problematic, offensive, and dehumanizing. Fostering inclusive learning environments for students with disabilities must be understood as a legal and ethical obligation and therefore a social justice issue rather than a financial opportunity to reconcile budget cuts. Further, reinforcing the misnomer that general education classrooms are the only way inclusion can truly occur within schools as a ruse to save money must also cease and desist since this practice is both unethical and dangerous.

## SCHOOL/PARENT RELATIONSHIPS

Currently, there is a chasm between what is discursively desired and what occurs in terms of relationships/interactions between parents of children with disabilities and schools. In order to address this chasm, the ways in which parents have been pathologized and subjected to coercive relations of power needs to be acknowledged and reconciled. Social capital (or a lack thereof) is a factor that shapes the ways in which parents of children with disabilities are responded to and as such, it is essential for biases in perceived capital to be recognized and actively rejected by those working with parents who have a child with a disability.

Reconceptualized relations and relationships with parents of children with disabilities will require that the field of education as a whole recognize assets parents have and thus, actively elicit knowledge about their children and the knowledge they have acquired while navigating systems that support their children. This approach to parents with children who have disabilities needs to be reflected in the professional literature available to educators as well so that is does not continue to validate and reinforce assimilative and coercive approaches and relationships. Respectful reciprocal interactions and relationships where all partners' knowledge is valued and seen as valuable is essential to successfully supporting a child who has a disability. Again, these ways of being are not only necessary to ensure attention to the rights of children with disabilities and their parents, but also so that ethically schools remain accountable to them.

## STRUCTURE AND PLANNING

The reconceptualization of disability, inclusion, responses to students with disabilities and their parents that has been developed throughout this book can be facilitated by a considered and methodical school wide plan. What is offered in Box 6.1 is a structured approach to facilitating reconceptualization processes at the school level. The phases are intended to allow for critical construction, deconstruction, and reconceptualization of thought, language, and practice in relation to students with disabilities and their parents to begin and become continuous within a school. What emerges throughout the three phases that are described can be recorded and thought of/used as data that can be researched by a school community to enrich and further the ongoing reconceptualization process. The outlined phases can also be applied at board of education or government levels and adapted to enable a critical examination of policies and official texts that organize disability and how people with disabilities are being responded to within the institutions these polices govern. The outlined phases and guiding questions are not intended as prescriptive directions that guarantee how reconceptualization is to be accomplished, but rather to provide a structure that focuses on and facilitates critical discussions, reflexivity, and planning to assist schools and educators in the ongoing process of reconceptualizing their thoughts and language about, and practices that respond to students with disabilities and their parents.

---

**Box 6.1 School Policy Development to Forward an Asset-Oriented Approach to Disability and Inclusion**

---

*Phase 1: Discussion of how the school and educators in it are constructing disability/students with disabilities and their parents.*
*Guiding questions:*

- *How are we thinking and talking about disability/students with disability and their parents?*
- *Where do these ideas and this language come from?*
- *What do these thoughts and language do for/to students with disabilities and their parents? How is it framing them?*

*Phase 2: Critical deconstruction of identity, pedagogy, placements and resources that are available to students with disabilities and their parents. Guiding questions:*

- *How are we responding to students with disabilities and their parents?*
- *How are thoughts and language about students with disabilities and their parents influencing how we are responding to them?*
- *How are these responses detrimental/beneficial to students with disabilities and their parents?*

*Phase 3: Reconceptualization of the identity, pedagogy, placements, and resources that are available to students with disabilities and their parents. Guiding Questions:*

- *What thoughts/language and practices ensure that students with disability and their parents are approached from an asset-oriented perspective?*
- *What pedagogies, placements, resources are available and in need of further developing to ensure that students with disabilities and their parents are responded to in ways that are asset-oriented?*
- *What are concrete demonstrations of changes that have been/can be made to pedagogies, placements and resources so that students with disabilities and their parents are approached in ways that are asset-oriented?*
- *What structures and strategies can be put in place to ensure that the reconceptualization of identity, pedagogy, placements, resources that are available to students with disabilities and their parents is ongoing and continuous?*

## "FINAL" THOUGHTS AND HOPES

The central aim of this book was to provide necessary critical discussion about questions, issues, and challenges facing educators while they attempt to support learners identified as having a disability within inclusive learning environments. Throughout my career as a teaching assistant, classroom and special education teacher, teacher educator, researcher, and curriculum course coordinator, these issues have become evident and in need of addressing in order for disability to be reconceptualized in ways that enable inclusion to be thoughtfully implemented. Continued critical discussions and planning are essential to ensure that students with disabilities are understood and provided for respectfully and responsively. I have offered these perspectives in order to invite this much-needed critical conversation. Ultimately my aim was to further develop an ethical and asset-oriented model of disability and inclusion in order to improve education for students with disabilities. In order to accomplish this, the book focused on reconceptualizing disability in education from its present discursive position as an inherent flaw to that of an asset, an epistemology, and an identity. In conjunction with destabilizing the monolith of disability as it appears in and is significant to education, the book explored pedagogies, practices, and possibilities that operationalize how education can respond to disability in ways that are genuinely inclusive.

What is integral to consider with respect to everything that is attempted and offered throughout this book is that it is neither prescriptive nor complete. A reconceptualization of disability is by its very nature open to revision. Pinar (1994) asserts that reconceptualization is never arrested and "to imagine it a finished product, a doctrine, is to miss the point. What is essential about the reconceptualization . . . is its constant redefinition" (p. 73). This book is therefore offered with the hope that it will further social justice–focused and equitable approaches to education as they relate to disability/students with disabilities and forward a critical reflexive monitoring and redefinition of what is understood about disability and done to/with students who have disabilities. This constant redefinition is critical to reconceptualist perspectives and approaches and as such, the book asks readers to engage with its content in ways that facilitate redefinition rather than subscription to doctrine or dogma. The ambitious task of developing and forwarding a reconceptualization of disability in education is ultimately pursued with the hope of exploring and creating new possibilities.

# References

Anderson, W., Chitwood, S., & Hayden, D. (1997). *Negotiating the special education maze: A guide for parents and teachers*. Bethesda, Md.: Woodbine House.

Bainbridge, J. & Heydon, R (2017). *Constructing Meaning: Teaching Language and Literacy K-8 (Sixth Edition.)*. Toronto, ON: Nelson Education Ltd.

Baker, B. (2002). The hunt for disability: The new eugenics and the normalization of school children. *Teachers College Record, 104*(4), 665–698

Bakhtin, M. M. (1981). *The dialogic imagination.* (C. Emerson & M. Holquist, Trans.). Austin, TX: University of Texas Press.

Barone, D. (2002). Literacy teaching in two kindergarten classrooms in a school labeled at-risk. *The Elementary School Journal*, 102 (5), 415–441

Belenky, M.F., Bond, L.A., Weinstock, J.S. (1997). Otherness. In M.F. Belenky, L.A. Bond & J.S. Weinstock (Eds.), *A tradition that has no name: Nurturing the development of people, families, and communities* (pp. 3–66). New York: Basic Books.

Bell, D.,& Jarvis, D. (2002). Letting go of 'letter of the week.' *Primary Voices K-6, 11*(2), 10–24.

Black, E. (2003). *War against the weak: Eugenics and America's campaign to create a master race*. New York: Four Walls Eight Windows.

Bouevitch, N. (2016, February 5). Parents resort to pulling special-needs children from resource starved schools. *The Globe and Mail*.

Bransford, J.D., & Johnson, M.K. (1972). Contextual prerequisites for understanding: Some investigations of comprehension and recall. *Journal of Verbal Learning and Verbal Behaviour, 11*, 717–726.

Brownlee, J., Schraw, G., & Berthelsen, D. (2011). Personal epistemology and teacher education. New York: NY: Routledge.

Burdell, P., & Swadener, B.B. (1999). Critical personal narrative and autoethnography in education: Reflections on a genre. *Educational Researcher, 28*, 21–26.

Burm, S. (2017). "Implementing policy is very complicated": Tracing the strategic and relational practices of the Ontario First Nation, Metis and Inuit educational policy framework through stories told by educators. Unpublished doctoral dissertation, University of Western Ontario.

Camborne, B. (1995). Toward an educationally relevant theory of literacy learning: Twenty years of Inquiry. *The Reading Teacher*, 49 (3), 182–190.

Camborne, B. (2000). Conditions for literacy learning: observing literacy learning in elementary classrooms: Nine years of classroom anthropology. *The Reading Teacher*, 56 (6), 512–515.

Camborne, B. (2001). Conditions for literacy learning: Turning learning theory into classroom instruction: A minicase study. *The Reading Teacher*, 54 (4), 414–417.

Camborne, B. (2002). Conditions for literacy learning: From conditions of learning to conditions of teaching. *The Reading Teacher*, 55 (4), 358–360.

Carlson, L. (2010). *The faces of intellectual disability: Philosophical reflections.* Bloomington, IN: Indiana University Press.

Clair, R.P. (2003).The changing story of ethnography. In R.P. Clair (Ed.), *Expressions of ethnography: Novel approaches to qualitative methods* (pp. 3–28). Albany, NY: State University of New York Press.

Clandinin, D.J., Murphy, S.M., Huber, J., & Orr, A.M. (2010). Negotiating narrative inquiries: Living in a tension filled midst. *The Journal of Educational Research,* 103, 81–90.

Comber, B. (2013). Critical Literacy in the Early Years: Emergence and Sustenance in an Age of Accountability. In Larson, Joanne & Marsh, Jackie (Eds.) *The SAGE Handbook of Early Childhood Literacy.* SAGE Publications, London, pp. 587–601.

Cope, B. & Kalantzis, M. (Eds.). (2000). *Multiliteracies: Literacy learning and the design of social futures*. London: Routledge.

Cummins, J. (2001). *Negotiating identities: Education for empowerment in a diverse society*. Los Angeles: California Association for Bilingual Education.

Cummins, J. (2005, April). *Diverse futures: Rethinking the image of the child in Canadian schools*. Presented at the Joan Pederson Distinguished Lecture Series, University of Western Ontario.

Cummins, J., & Early, M. (2015). *Big ideas for expanding minds: Teaching English Language learners across the curriculum.* Oakville, ON: Rubicon Publishing.

Curwin, R. (2012). Parents and teachers: the possibility of a dream team. *Edutopia.* Retrieved at: https://www.edutopia.org/blog/parent-teacher-collaboration-richard-curwin.

Danforth, S. (2009). *The incomplete child: An intellectual history of learning disabilities*. New York: Peter Lang.

Davis, L. (1997). Constructing normalcy. In L. Davis (ed.), *The disability studies reader*. New York: Routledge.

Dean, H. (1992). Poverty discourse and the disempowerment of the poor. *Critical Social Policy*, 12 (35), 79–88.

Delpit, L. (2003). Educators as "Seed People" growing a new future. *Educational Researcher*, 32 (7), 14–21.

DeLuca, S. (2000). *Finding meaning places for healing: Toward a vigilant subjectivity in the practice of a nurse educator.* Unpublished doctoral dissertation, University of Toronto, Canada.

Dessemontet, R.S., & Bless, G. (2013). The impact of including children with intellectual disability in general education classrooms on the academic achievement of their low, average, and high-achieving peers. *Journal of Intellectual & Developmental Disability*, 38(1), 23–30.

Dolmage, J. T. (2014). *Disability rhetoric.* Syracuse, NY: Syracuse University Press.

Dudley-Marling, C. (2004). The social construction of learning disabilities. *Journal of Learning Disabilities, 37 (6)*, 482–489.

Edwards, K. (2005). *The memory keeper's daughter.* New York City, NY: Viking Press.

Fraser, F.G., & Shields, C.M. (2010). Leaders' roles in disrupting dominant discourses and promoting inclusion. In A.L. Edmunds & R.B. Macmillan (Eds.), *Leadership for inclusion: A practical guide* (pp. 7–18). Rotterdam: Sense Publishers.

Gardner, H. (1983). *Frames of Mind.* New York: Basic Book Inc.

Gee, J.P. (2001). A sociocultural perspective on early literacy development. In S.B. Newman, D.K. Dickinson (Eds.), *Handbook of early literacy research* (pp. 30–42). New York: Guilford Press.

Gentry, J. (2016). An auto/biographical narrative: A critical reflection on learning with dyslexia. *Vitae Scholasticae: The Journal of Educational Biography, 33 (2)*, 19–35.

Goodley, D. (2007). Towards socially just pedagogies: Deleuzoguattarian critical disability studies. *International Journal of Inclusive Education, 11* (3), 318.

Graham, B. & Iannacci, L. (2013). Reconceptualizing "Special Education" Curriculum in a Bachelor of Education Program: Teacher Candidate Discourses and Teacher Educator Practices. *Canadian Journal of Disability Studies.* 2(2):10–34.

Granger, C. (2004). *Silence in second language learning: A psychoanalytic reading.* Great Britain: Multilingual Matters Ltd.

Grant, C. A. (1999) Introduction: The idea, the invitation, and chapter themes. In C. A.Grant (Ed.). *Multicultural research: A reflective engagement with race, class, gender and sexual orientation.* Philadelphia: Falmer.

Gregory (2004). *Psychological Testing: History, Principles, and Applications*, 4th Edition. London, England: Pearson.

Halliday, M.A.K. (1975). *Learning how to mean: Explorations in the functions of language.* London, UK: Edward Arnold.

Harman, B. (2009). *Inclusion/Integration: Is there a difference?* Proceeding from the 10th World Down Syndrome Congress, Dublin City University, Dublin, Ireland. August 19th–22nd, 2009.

Harpell, J.V., & Andrews J.J.W. (2010). Administrative leadership in the age of inclusion: Promoting best practices and teacher empowerment. *The Journal of Educational Thought, 44*(2), 189–210.

Hehir, T. (2002). Eliminating ableism in education. *Harvard Educational Review*, 72 (1), 1–32.

Herda, E.A. (1999*). Research conversations and narrative: A critical hermeneutic orientation in participatory inquiry.* Wesport, CT: Praeger.

Heydon R., & Iannacci, L. (2008). *Early childhood curricula and the de-pathologizing of childhood.* Toronto, ON: University of Toronto Press.

Hibbert, K. (2013). Finding wisdom in practice: The genesis of the Salty Chip, A Canadian multiliteracies collaborative. *Language and Literacy, 15*(1), 29.

Hornberger, N. (2000). Multilingual literacies, literacy practices, and the continua of biliteracy. In Martin-Jones & K. Jones (Eds.), *Multilingual literacies* (pp. 353–369). Amsterdam/Philadelphia: John Benjamins Pub. Co.

Hosking, D.L. (2008, September 2–4). Critical disability theory. *Paper presented at the 4th disability studies conference.* Lancaster University, UK.

Iannacci, L. (2005). *Othered among others: A critical narrative of culturally and linguistically diverse (CLD) learners' literacy and identity in early childhood education (ECE).* Unpublished doctoral dissertation, The University of Western Ontario, London, Ontario, Canada.

Iannacci, L. (2007). Learning to "Do" School: Procedural display and culturally and linguistically diverse (CLD) students in Canadian early childhood education (ECE). *Journal of the Canadian Association for Curriculum Studies, 4 (2)*, 55–76.

Iannacci, L. (2008). The pathologizing of culturally and linguistically diverse students in early-years classrooms. In R. Heydon R., & L. Iannacci, L. (2008). *Early childhood curricula and the de-pathologizing of childhood,* pp. 46–81. Toronto, ON: University of Toronto Press.

Iannacci, L., & Whitty P. (Eds.). (2009). *Early childhood curricula: Reconceptulist perspectives.* Calgary, AL: Detselig Enterprises Ltd.

Iannacci, L. (2018). Impoverished Pedagogy: A critical examination of assumptions about poverty, teaching and cultural and linguistic diversity. In Harkins, M.J., & Singer, S. (Eds.). *Educators on Diversity, Social Justice, and Schooling: A Reader.* Canadian Scholars Press.

Iannacci, L., Muia, F., Porco, M. (2018). Reconceptualizing Inclusion: A Critical Exploration for Educators. In Smale, W. (Ed.). *Perspectives on Educational Law and Policy.* Word & Deed Publishing.

Jordan, A., Schwartz, E., & McGhie-Richmond, D. (2010). The supporting effective teaching (SET) Project: The Relationship of inclusive teaching practices to teachers' beliefs about disability and ability, and about their roles as teachers. *Teacher and Teacher Education,* 26 (2), 259–266.

Jordan, A., & Stanovich, P. (2003). Teachers' personal epistemological beliefs about students with disabilities as indicators of effective teaching practices. *Journal of Research in Special Educational Needs,* 3 (1), 1–14.

Kim, E., & Aquino, K.C. (2017). *Disability as diversity in higher education.* New York, NY: Routledge.

Kliewer, C., Biklen, D., & Kasa-Hendrickson, C. (2006). Who may be literate? Disability and resistance to the cultural denial of competence. *American Educational Research Journal,* 43 (2), 163–167

Kunc, N. (1992). *The need to belong: rediscovering Maslow's hierarchy of needs.* Retrieved February 19, 2016, from: http://www.broadreachtraining.com/articles/armaslow.htm.

Lieblich, A., Tuval-Mashiach, R., Zilber, T. (1998). *Narrative Research*: Reading, analysis and interpretation. California: Sage Publications.

Lloyd, S. (1992). *The Jolly Phonics Handbook*. UK: Jolly Learning.

McDermott, R., & Varenne, H. (1995). Culture as disability. *Anthropology and Education Quarterly, 26*(3), 323–325.

McLaren, A. (1990). *Our own master race: Eugenics in Canada, 1885–1945*. Toronto: McClelland & Stewart.

Meyer, L.M. (2000). Barriers to meaningful instruction for English learners. *Theory into Practice, 39*(4), 228–236.

Miller, J. (1998). Autobiography and the Necessary Incompleteness of Teachers' Stories. In W. Ayers & J. Miller (Eds.), *A light in dark times: Maxine Greene and the unfinished conversation* (pp. 145–154). New York: Teachers College Press.

Moffatt, L. (2006). *(Dis)abling readers: Discourses of literacy and learning in research on "Reading disabilities" 2000–2005*. Unpublished dissertation comprehensive exam. University of British Columbia.

Moll, L. (1992). Funds of knowledge for teaching: Using a qualitative approach to connect homes and classrooms. *Theory into Practice, 31* (2), 132–41.

Moss, G. (2004). Provisions of trustworthiness in critical narrative research: Bridging intersubjectivity and fidelity. *The Qualitative Report, 9* (2), 363.

Munyi, C.W. (2012). Past and present perceptions of disability: A historical perspective. *Disability Studies Quarterly, 32* (2). 1–10.

National Council on Disability (2015). *Breaking the school-to-prison pipeline for students with disabilities*. Washington, DC.

New London Group, (1996). A pedagogy of multiliteracies: Designing social futures. *Harvard Educational Review, 66* (1), 60–92.

Obiakor, F.E., Harris, M., Mutua, K., Rotatori, A., & Algozzine B. (2012). Making inclusion work in general education classrooms. *Education & Treatment of Children, 35* (3), 482–483.

Odom, S.L., Parrish, T.B., & Hikido, C. (2001). The costs of inclusive and traditional Special education preschool services. *Journal of Special Education Leadership. 14* (1), 33–41.

Ontario Ministry of Education. (2015). *Special Education Funding Guidelines: Special Incidence Portion (SIP)*, 2015–2016.

Ontario Psychological Association. (2010*). Sharing promising practices resource guide: Kindergarten to grade four*.

Patton, M.Q. (2002). *Qualitative research & evaluation measures (3rd edition)*. Thousand Oaks; California: Sage.

Paugh, P. C., & Dudley-Marling, C. (2011). 'Speaking' deficit into (or out of) existence: How language constrains classroom teachers' knowledge about instructing diverse learners. *International Journal of Inclusive Education*, 1–15.

Pinar, W. (1994). *Autobiography, politics and sexuality: Essays in curriculum theory 1972–1992*. New York: Peter Lang.

Pothier, D., & Devlin, R. (2006). Introduction: Toward a critical theory of dis-citizenship. In D. Pothier & R. Devlin (Eds.), *Critical disability theory: Essays in philosophy, politics, policy, and law*. Vancouver, BC: UBC Press.

Reay, D. (1998). *Class work: Mothers' involvement in their children's primary schooling*. London: Routledge.

Rich, S.J. (1998). *Reading for meaning in the elementary school*. Toronto: ITP Nelson.

Ricoeur, P. (1992*). Oneself as another*. Chicago, IL: University of Chicago Press.

Roth, K. (2015). Commit to inclusion confusion. *Journal of Physical Education, Recreation & Dance, 86* (3), 3–4.

Routman, R. (2000). *Conversations: Strategies for teaching, learning and evaluating*. Portsmouth, NH: Heinemann.

Schwartz, E., & Jordan, A., (2011). Teachers' epistemological beliefs and practices with students with disabilities and at-risk in inclusive classrooms: Implications for teacher development. In J. Brownlee, G. Schraw & D. Berthelsen. *Personal epistemology and teacher education*, pp. 210–226. New York: NY: Routledge.

Shields, C.M., Bishop, R., & Mazawi, A.E. (2005*). Pathologizing practices: The impact of deficit thinking on education*. New York: Peter Lang.

Strickland, D. (1998). What's basic in beginning reading? Finding common ground. *Educational Leadership*. 55 (6), 6–10.

Strickland, D.S. (1994). Reinventing our literacy programs: Books, basics, balance. *The Reading Teacher*, 48, 294–302.

Swadener, B.B., & Lubeck, S. (1995). (Eds.*). Children and families "at Promise:" Deconstructing the discourse of risk*. Albany, NY: Albany State University of New York Press.

Titchosky, T. (2007). *Reading and writing disability differently*. Toronto, ON: University of Toronto Press.

Thomas, C. (2004). How is disability understood? An examination of sociological approaches. Disability & Society, 19 (6). 570–583

Toohey, K. (2000). *Learning English at school: Identity, social relations and classroom practice*. Great Britain: Multilingual Matters Ltd.

Torgesen, J. K., & Mathes, P. G. (1999). Assessment and instruction in phonological awareness. Florida Department of Education Reprint. Retrieved from: http://www.fldoe.org/core/fileparse.php/7690/urlt/0070131-phonoman.pdf

Triplett, C. F. (2007). The social construction of "Struggle": Influences of school literacy contexts, curriculum, and relationships. *Journal of Literacy Research, 39*(1), 95–126.

Viruru, R., & Cannella, G.S., (2001). Postcolonial ethnography, young children, and voice. In S. Grieshaber & G. Cannella, (Ed.), *Embracing identities in early childhood education; Diversity and possibilities* (p. 168). New York: Teachers College Press.

Vygotsky, L. (1978*). Mind and society: The development of higher psychological processes*. Cambridge, MA: Harvard University Press.

Warnock, B.M., (2010, September 17). The cynical betrayal of my special needs children. *The Telegraph*. UK. pp.1–2.

Winzer, M. (2008). *Children with exceptionalities in Canadian classrooms 8th (ed.).* Toronto, ON: Pearson Education Canada.

Woodill, G.A. (1992). International early childhood care and education: Historical Perspectives. In G. Woodill, J. Bernhard, L. Prochner (ed.), *International handbook of early childhood education.* (p. 7). New York: Garland Publishing.

Wyndham, J. (1955). *The chrysalids.* Great Britain: Penguin Books.

Yin, R.K. (2009). Case study research: Design and methods (4th Ed.) Thousand Oaks, CA: Sage.

Yuknis, C., & Bernstein, E.R.. (2017). Supporting students with non-disclosed disabilities. In E, Kim & K. C. Aquino, K.C. (2017). *Disability as diversity in higher education.* New York, NY: Routledge.

# Index

# About the Author

Dr. Luigi Iannacci is an Associate Professor in the School of Education and Professional Learning at Trent University in Peterborough, Ontario, Canada. He teaches and coordinates courses that focus on special needs students and language and literacy teaching and learning. He has taught mainstream and special education in a range of elementary grades in Ontario, Canada. His research interests and publications are focused on critical dis/ability studies, first and second language and literacy learning, critical multiculturalism, early childhood education, critical narrative research and ethics. He is the past president of LLRC (Language and Literacy Researchers of Canada) and the ISEB (International Society for Educational Biography).

Dr. Iannacci can be reached at luigiiannacci@trentu.ca.
Website: http://people.trentu.ca/luigiiannacci/index.html

Lightning Source UK Ltd.
Milton Keynes UK
UKHW010037110120
356744UK00001B/20/P